THEOLOGICAL and NATURAL SCIENCE

By

Thomas F. Torrance

Wipf and Stock Publishers
Eugene, Oregon

Theological and Natural Science
By T. F. Torrance
Copyright 2002 by T. F. Torrance

ISBN: 1-57910-790-7

Wipf and Stock Publishers
199 West 8th Avenue
Eugene, OR 97401

To my dear Wife

Margaret Edith Torrance

and our dear sons and daughter

Thomas Spear Torrance,
Iain Richard Torrance,
and
Alison Meta Elizabeth Torrance

in boundless love and gratitude

Contents

Preface

This book represents a selection of my later lectures and addresses on interrelations between Christian theology and natural science, especially as I delved more deeply into the writings and thinking of James Clerk Maxwell, and then turned back to study the remarkable thought of John Philoponos of Alexandria, the sixth century theologian and physicist of the great Academy in Alexandria. My concern was the interrelation between theological and scientific thinking that had developed there from the second to the sixth century. In my earlier years I had concentrated on the thought of Einstein and Plank aroused when, on the recommendation of Norman Kemp Smith, I read Max Planck's work, *Where is Science Going*? In mid-stream I became fascinated with the Gifford Lectures of Michael Polanyi who took me to his heart after he read my work *Theological Science*, and we became warm friends. After the Vatican Council I was one of the founding members of the International Academy of Theological Science and soon joined its sister institution the International Academy of the Philosophy of Science, both established by Stanislas Dockx, OP, in Brussels at the end of the Vatican Council. It was through the latter particularly that I had the privilege of getting to know some of the leading scientists and mathematicians in Europe, such as Ilya Prigogine, Olivier Costa de Beauregard, Bernard d'Espagnat, Paulette Fevrier, J-L Destouches, André Mercier, I. Gonseth, Giuseppe Del Re, Paul Gochet, Sir John Eccles then in Switzerland, and the great John Archibald Wheeler who joined us from Princeton. Giuseppe Del Re from Rome and Naples and I were also original members of the International Academy for Environmental Questions, founded and directed by the remarkable Helmut Metzner of Tübingen. Del Re became deeply influenced, as I was, by James Clerk Maxwell's work *A Treatise on Electricity & Magnetism*, which as Einstein claimed had radically altered the axiomatic structure of science. I was particularly influenced not only by Clerk Maxwell's light theory but by his analysis and development of scientific method in his great work *A Treatise on Electricity and Magnetism*, which ranks with Newton's *Principia Mathematica* in the foundations of natural science.

When in 1982 Edinburgh University and the Royal Society of Edinburgh were commemorating the fourth centenary of the University of Edinburgh and the second centenary of the Royal Society of Edinburgh, I was horrified to find that they seemed to be overlooking the great work of James Clerk Maxwell. And so I extracted from his Scientific Papers, and published for the first time in a separate form, his epoch making work, *A Dynamical Theory of the Electromagnetic Field*, and dedicated it both to Edinburgh University and the Royal Society of Edinburgh. It has now also been published by Wipf & Stock, in

Oregon, USA. The new physics building in Edinburgh University has now been named after Clerk Maxwell, and a research unit dedicated to Clerk Maxwell has been established in India Street, Edinburgh, headed by Professor David Ritchie, devoted to Clerk Maxwellian mathematics as well as physics.

During my participation in the Faith and Order Movement of the World Council of Churches I met and had discussions with Armenian and so-called Monophysite churchman and theologians and realized that their Christology was in reality far from being heterodox, as claimed by Greek Orthodox and Roman Catholic theologians, and was in fact very close to the teaching of the Council of Chalcedon of decisive importance for Greek and Roman Churches alike. I came to realize that the mischief lay in the rather Aristotelian slant after the Council of Chalcedon in 451 that had been given by the so-called "orthodox" understanding by Greek Orthodox and Roman Catholic theologians alike, of the formula of the Chalcedonian Council about the divine and human natures of Christ. This led me to give deeper critical attention to the contrast drawn by theologians and churchmen between the Alexandrian and Antiochene doctrine of Christ, and in particular to the relation between the teaching of Cyril of Alexandria and Severus of Antioch. My understanding was later to be greatly reinforced by the Oxford dissertation of my son Iain, *Christology After Chalcedon, Severus of Antioch and Sergius the Monophysite* (1998).

This prompted me to give serious attention to the writings of John Philoponos of Alexandria, the sixth century theologian and scientist in his adherence to the teaching of Athanasius and Cyril of Alexandria, and in his trenchant critique of Aristotelian physics, which yielded his astonishing anticipation of Clerk Maxwellian science. Alas, however, when John Philoponos gave a more dynamic theological interpretation of the teaching of Cyril of Alexandria, he was anathematized by the Aristotelian churchmen in Byzantium. That had the disastrous effect of retarding the advance of science for more than a thousand years.

My interest in and study of the works of John Philoponos were greatly quickened by the writings of Professor S. Sambursky, the Jewish scientist, whose scientist brother, Benjamin, was murdered by Japanese terrorists at Lod Airport in Israel. I got to know Professor S. Sambursky in 1976 when he was the President of the Hebrew University in Jerusalem. He directed me to study Philoponos' theory of light, and pointed to the work of Walter Böhm, *Johannes Philoponos Grammatikos von Alexandrien,* 1967. A former student of mine, Dr George Dragas, now Professor in Hellenic College in Massachussetts, helped me to acquire some of the Greek texts of Philoponos' works, in particular the *De Opificio Mundi*, his commentary on St Basil's work on the creation.

One day in 1975, in the weekly discussions by Philosophers in Edinburgh University, when I referred to John Philoponos, Dr Sarah Waterlow (who as Sarah Broadie was to become Professor of Aristotelian Philosophy in Princeton), told me of the interest in the thought of John Philoponos by Richard Sorabji of King's College London. He and some of his friends have since been publishing a number of works dealing with John Philoponos, through the Duckworth Press in London. When delivering the Payton lectures on *Reality and Scientific Theology* in Pasadena in 1981, and discussing with postgraduate students the thought of John Philoponos, I met John Emory McKenna a Princeton graduate in physics (taught by John Archibald Wheeler), when he was teaching Hebrew at Fuller Theological Seminary. When I spoke about the importance of Philoponos, and the need to translate some of his works which were extant only in Syriac, he responded to my call, learned Syriac and eventually wrote a doctoral dissertation (examined by Sebastian Brock) on *The Arbiter*. In Dr McKenna's edition of that work, now published by Wipf & Stock, John Philoponos is shown to be no monophysite but an orthodox Christian theologian, as well as an innovating scientist.

The ancient theologian from whom I have learned most and value above all others in the foundations he laid for all Christendom, was Athanasius the Great of Alexandria. But it was when I discovered the writings of John Philoponos that I learned in a newer and deeper way the fertile impact of Christian thinking, and Alexandrian theology in particular, not only upon the advance of human life and thought in general but upon the foundations of natural science and our scientific understanding of the world created through the mighty Word of God incarnate in the Lord Jesus Christ. It was particularly in studying the thought and writing of John Philoponos Professor in the great Academy of Alexandria that I discerned the powerful heuristic impact of Christian theology upon the foundations and advance of natural science and of physics in particular. It was not the ancient philosophy, Aristotelian, Platonic and Stoic, taught in Alexandria, that enabled Philoponos to achieve his "break through", but the Athanasian and Basilian doctrine of the creation of the universe out nothing and the contingent nature of its rational order through the dynamic Word of God that shaped his scientific understanding. That is what we find in Philoponos' work *De Opificio Mundi*, a theologico-scientific or philosophical commentary on Basil's account of creation under the guidance of the opening statements of the Book of Genesis. It was the biblical teaching about the role of the Word and Light of God in creation that fascinated John Philoponos so that he gave it primary place in the development of his scientific understanding of the contingent order of the created universe. What became very clear to me as I studied the works of Philoponos was the impact of biblical and Christian theology in the formation and development of scientific theory. Thus I liked to think of his science pursued in this distinctive way as "theological science". That is to say, his theology had a direct as well as a regulative impact on his heuristic scientific thinking, his discoveries and development in natural science. That is what I had already found in the epoch-making advance of physical and mathematical natural science in the work of the great James Clerk Maxwell. And so I like to think of John Philoponos of Alexandria in the sixth century as a forerunner of James Clerk Maxwell of Edinburgh.

This collection of essays largely comprises addresses on the thought of Clerk Maxwell and John Philoponos. But they begin with a lecture I was due to give (but prevented by illness from giving) in Washington, DC, at the invitation of my former student Lloyd Ogilvie, Chaplain to the US Senate, and of James H. Billington, Congress Librarian. Along with the essays on Clerk Maxwell and

John Philoponos, I have included one on Einstein delivered at the Center of Theological Inquiry in Princeton, reprinted from *Reflections*, Volume I, Spring 1998; one on Michael Polanyi contributed to *Tradition & Discovery. The Polanyi Society Journal*, vol. XXIV, vol.1, 1997-98; and my contribution to *John Paul II On Science and Religion, Reflections on the New View From Rome 1990*.

Several of my essays and lectures on John Philoponos reproduced here overlap in their argument and content, as they were delivered in lectures in different institutions and places where I was trying to direct attention to Philoponos. However instead of reducing them, I have left them as they were originally composed or delivered. I make no apology for that, for what we now learn about the scientific and theological contributions of Philoponos needs to be carefully assimilated today in theological and scientific thought alike.

I am greatly indebted to my elder son Thomas Spear Torrance for his considerable help in computing and in preparation of this volume.

Thomas F. Torrance
Edinburgh, Scotland,
2nd October 2001

Chapter 1

Theological Science and Scientific Theology, in History and Today

I believe that there is a deep cognitive relation between theology and natural science, if only because, as James Clerk Maxwell and Albert Einstein both in their different ways, there is and indeed must be a fundamental harmony between the laws of the mind and the laws of nature, an inherent relation between how we think and how nature behaves independently of our minds. The more profoundly our scientific understanding penetrates into the rational order of the universe of space and time, the more clearly and fully that pre-established harmony between the mind and nature becomes manifest, and also between the Creator and man. This surely applies to the interrelations between a scientific theology and natural science. They are concerned in different ways with the kind of intelligibility immanent in the created universe - that is with the contingent rational order with which all empirical and theoretical sciences have to do and upon which they are grounded. My concern, here, however, is not just with methodological relations between them, but with the conceptual interface between them, for I believe that rigorously pursued Christian theology and natural science contribute positively to one another, and that the reciprocal impact between them is much more profound and heuristically important than is usually realized by theologians and scientists. That is why here I speak of science developed in this rigorous way as "theological science" (i.e. theologically influenced science), and of Christian theology strictly pursued as "scientific theology" (scientifically influenced theology).

Let me begin by referring to what took place in the first six centuries when Christian thinkers laid the foundations upon which all subsequent empirical and theoretical science has developed. It was in Alexandria that decisive changes were made. There at the turn of the first century scientists arose who were dissatisfied with trying to understand the world in *a priori* abstract theoretical forms in Platonic, Aristotelian, or Stoic ways. They set about developing a new kind of open inquiry in which they asked positive questions or framed "thought experiments" designed to disclose the nature of the realities into which they inquired. These natural scientists, called *physikoi*, were sharply attacked by skeptical thinkers like Sextus Empiricus who called them *dogmatikoi* - not because they were dogmatic in the later sense of that term but because they were concerned to ask questions that might yield true answers under the positive or dogmatic constraint of nature.

The *physikoi* regarded science as proceeding strictly in accordance with nature, *kata physin*, in order to bring to light the actual nature of any reality under question. This was called *dogmatike episteme* or dogmatic science in which scientific thinking was pursued faithfully under the constraint of what the nature of something really is, and allowed the conceptual assent of the mind to that reality, as it becomes progressively disclosed to it, to determine how they are to think truly of it and express their understanding of it. This scientific method of inquiry (ἡ μέθοδος τῆς εὑρέσεως) was held to apply in every field of knowledge, when an appropriate modality of the reason would be developed under the constraint of the specific nature of the object and the information it yielded.

That was the intellectual milieu in which early Christian thinkers like Clement of Alexandria in the second/third century sought to think out and commend their faith. It was in Alexandria that scientific and theological thinking began to flow together and theology and science interacted with one another, conceptually, epistemologically, and even linguistically, within the same unitary world of space and time so that careful attention had to be given to the whole created order, as it came from God and as it is sustained by his creative Word. And it was there in the Great Academy of Alexandria that careful scientific theological inquiry concerned with the nature and activity of God was developed by the great theologians of the early Church such as Athanasius, and Cyril who spoke of Christian theology as *dogmatike episteme*, or dogmatic science, in which they allowed the nature and activity of God, as he is revealed to mankind through his *Logos* or Word incarnate in Jesus Christ, to determine how they were to think of him. Owing to the fact that immense attention was devoted to the doctrines of the creation and of the incarnation within the created order of space and time, a radical transformation within the foundations of knowledge and in cosmological outlook took place, to which our modern empirical and theoretical science is indebted.

Under the impact of that Christian theology in Alexandria there arose a new scientific conception of the universe of space and time as *contingent* (ἐνδέχομενος, an Aristotelian term re-minted and brought into play by Athanasius) in nature and its rational order which pointed, not necessarily or accidentally, but freely beyond itself to God, the ultimate ground, cause and reason, the ultimate *why* of all the contingent natural order. By its very nature this contingent universe is incomplete (ἀκατασκεύαστος). Far from being self-sufficient or self-explanatory, the universe points beyond itself to the transcendent ground of intelligibility in the Logos or rational Word of God incarnate in Jesus Christ in the time and space of this world.

In that transformation attention must be given to three basic factors.

1. The Judaeo-Christian doctrine of the one God, the Creator of all things visible and in visible, questioned Greek polytheism and pluralism, polymorphism, hylomorphism, and dualism, and demanded a unitary conception of the created universe which called for a scientific way of research and knowledge that answered to its rational order.

2. The biblical view of the goodness of the creation, reinforced by the doctrine of the incarnation of the eternal Word of God within the creation, destroyed the idea that sensible and empirical events are not accessible to rational thought, and established instead the reality of the empirical world in the recognition that temporal and sensible realities have a common rationality of a contingent kind, open to scientific investigation and understanding.

3. The fact that God himself in creating the universe out of nothing has conferred upon it one comprehensive rational order, dependent on his own, had the effect of destroying the Aristotelian and Ptolemaic separation between the sensible and intelligible worlds and so between terrestrial and celestial mechanics, and at the same time gave rise to dynamic and relational concepts of space and time as bearers of rational order in the universe.

That was the Christian view of God and the universe which John Philoponos, scientist and theologian of Alexandria in the sixth century, inherited, and set himself to develop and defend against Neo-Platonist and Aristotelian attacks, and on the basis of which to deepen and develop scientific and theological understanding of the created order. As an astronomer he composed a treatise on the *Astrolabe*, a complicated astronomical instrument, the oldest to survive from the ancient world. Then he turned to clarify epistemological issues at stake in contemporary philosophy and science, and became a powerful scientific thinker of remarkable insight who combined empirical and theoretic ways of scientific inquiry evident not least in his critical examination of the prevailing Ptolemaic cosmology and Aristotelian physics. Throughout his life he set himself in particular to carry through a comprehensive examination of the works of Aristotle, and developed a powerful critique of his physics and cosmology, in the course of which he injected into the stream of European thought revolutionary scientific ideas that anticipated those of Clerk Maxwell and Albert Einstein.

My concern now is to show something of the heuristic force of Christian theology in the scientific advance made by John Philoponos and Clerk Maxwell, and to justify the claim that the positive impact of Christian theology and natural science upon one another is rather more subtle, profound and important than is usually realized by theologians and scientists.

1. *John Philoponos "Grammatikos" or Professor at the great Academy of philosophy and science at Alexandria.*

The theology of John Philoponos was biblical and Christocentric, in line with that of Athanasius, Cyril, and Severus of Antioch, in which he developed the Christian conception of the creation of the universe and its rational order out of nothing. His thinking moved from a firm base in Biblical and Nicene theology into physics, dynamics, optics, meteorology and cosmology, and then back into theology in such a way that his theological thinking and his scientific thinking affected, fertilized and deepened one another. His science cannot be adequately understood in abstraction from his theology, while his theology may not be appreciated except in the epistemological depth and precision it gained from his critical and creative engagement with traditional Hellenistic philosophy and science. Of central importance was the way in which he brought the Hebraeo-Christian doctrine of mighty living God and the creation of the universe of space and time out of nothing to bear in sharp criticism upon Neoplatonic and Aristotelian notions of the eternity of the world. Although many of Philoponos' main works were destroyed or lost, we are able to recover a good deal of his scientific thought from the massive *Commentaries of Simplicius*, the Aristotelian philosopher, who sought to confute him. I shall also take into in account several of Philoponos' works which have survived intact, particularly, *De aeternitate mundi contra Proclum, De aeternitate mundi contra Aristotelem*, together with his biblical account of the creation of the world, *De Opificio Mundi*, and the *Arbiter* or *Diatetes*. The science of John Philoponos is not to be understood in abstraction from his theology, while his theology may not be appreciated except in the epistemological depth and precision gained from his conflict with Greek philosophy and science. They had a profound epistemological and dynamic impact upon each other.

In recent years helpful work has been devoted to the writing and thinking of Philoponos, to which I am indebted. I refer particularly to that of Samuel Sambursky, *The Physical World of Late Antiquity*, 1962; of Walter Böhm, *Johannes Philoponos, Grammatikos von Alexandrien. Ausgewälte Schriften*, 1962; and particularly to Richard Sorabji: *Philoponus and the rejection of Aristotelian science*, 1987; *The Arbiter of John Philoponos*, by John McKenna, 1998. Under the guidance of Richard Sorabji a corpus of Philoponos' works is in process of being published, but the interest of most of those engaged in that enterprise seems to me to bear more on Aristotelian philosophy than on theology and science.

One cannot read Philoponos' work on the creation of the world, *De opificio mundi,* without realizing the importance he attached to the biblical account of the origin of the universe through the creative Word of God which he regarded from a Christological perspective. In Jesus Christ the Wisdom and creative Word of all things (ὁ τῶν ὅλων δημιουργὸς λόγος) became incarnate, through whom information is mediated which we would not otherwise have, but under the guidance of which genuinely scientific account of the world of space and time may be worked out. It was this theological understanding of the created rational order of the universe of space and time that provided him with a grasp of the actual contingent nature of the universe, and helped him to put forward a genuine scientific understanding of the empirical laws of its rational order. Here theological information which was not and could not be gained through natural science itself nevertheless played a positive and effective role in the development of scientific inquiry.

This is very evident in the special importance Philoponos gave to the biblical and theological account of the creation of *light* through the majestic fiat of the divine Logos. "Let there be light, and there was light". That distinction between the uncreated Light, which God himself is, and created light, like that between the creative Spirit of God and created spirit, exercised a major role not only in his theology but in his science, for it called for fresh thinking about the physics of light, which he undertook in controversial examination of Aristotle's static notion of light put forward in his *De Anima*.

In contrast Philoponos put forward a conception of light as a real activity, an immaterial invisible dynamic force which moves directionally and continuously at a timeless or unlimited velocity (ταχεῖα...ἤ ἄχρονος). This concept of light as dynamic incorporeal activity which he called "light force" (φωστικὴ δύναμις), had far-reaching implications for optics, physics and dynamics: it involved a new kinetic theory (κινητική τις δύναμις ἀσώματος, ἐνέργειά τις ἀσώματος κινητική) in sharp antithesis to that of Aristotle. What Philoponos did then, taking his cue from the kinetic propagation of light, was in fact to propound a new theory of impetus, on the analogy between the impetus imparted to a projectile in being hurled and the incorporeal force or momentum in the movement of light imparted to it by the Creator. Philoponos' light theory and impetus theory together amounted to a radical rejection of Aristotelian physics and mechanics and registered an immense advance in scientific understanding of the universe approaching that of modern times. This combination of light theory and impetus theory was congenial, as Philoponos realized, to the Christian understanding of the creation of the universe out of nothing, for God himself is the source of all matter and form, and all light and energy in the universe. Thus Philoponos' light theory and impetus theory together scientifically reinforced and contributed to the unitary view of heaven and earth, matter and form, space and time, freely created by God Almighty out of nothing. It was through the eternal Word incarnate in Jesus Christ, the Light of the World, that God has freely endowed space and time with their active force (κινητικὴ δύναμις) and continues to maintain and hold them together in their rational order.

The combination of Philoponos's dynamic and relational theories of light and motion reinforced the open-structured notions of space and time already developed by theologians, and gave rise to a conception of the universe governed throughout by an internal cohesion affecting and unifying all activity within it. Thus light theory and impetus theory constituted together a kind of dynamic field theory (ἕξις τις) of light, in astonishing anticipation of that of James Clerk Maxwell in the nineteenth century. The immediate effect of this in the fifth and sixth centuries was to liberate science from the closed mechanical world of Aristotle, nowhere more apparent than in his quantitative notion of space as the immobile limit within which a body is contained, and to replace it with a relational open-structured kind of rational order. Moreover, this change in the conception of space applied, *mutatis mutandis*, also to Philoponos' relational conception of time in the reciprocal bearing of time and motion upon one another.

All this had the effect of profoundly altering the fundamental conception of the nature (φύσις) of things, and consequently of the understanding of scientific inquiry as pursued strictly "in accordance with the nature (κατὰ φύσιν) of things, that is, in accordance with what things really and actually are (κατ' ἀλήθειαν), and therefore in accordance with their dynamic nature and natural force (κατὰ τὴν φυσικὴν δύναμιν). This change toward a radically dynamic and relational conception of the inherent order and nature of the universe of space and time imported a basic change in the pursuit of objective scientific inquiry itself, and correspondingly in the precise meaning and handling of scientific terms. That was nowhere more apparent than in the dynamic conception and meaning of "nature" or φύσις itself, and of reality or ἀλήθεια, for example, in their frequent synonymous relation to one another, which the Aristotelians failed to appreciate.

Let us return again to the contrast between Aristotle's static notion of light and Philoponos' dynamic understanding and relational conception of light, for what was involved was a contrast between thinking in abstract logical relations and in real dynamic relations. Philoponos realized that Aristotelian logic applied only to static relations or idealized forms, as in Euclidean geometry, and not to real intelligible relations in the actual dynamic world of space and time. Hence he deliberately moved away from abstract thinking in terms of logical analysis and syllogistic argumentation, toward a holistic and dynamical mode of inquiry in accordance with the dynamic nature of the reality and movement of light. Of particular significance here was his way of conceiving of the whole and the parts, in science and theology alike, and the critical handling of formal-logical solutions, in the face of Aristotelian analysis and logic, in favor of real intelligible relations rather than logico-analytical relations. This was a move away from abstract thought, from logicalist analysis and argumentation, toward a holistic and dynamical mode of inquiry in accordance with the inherent intelligibility and the dynamic nature of light, in which primacy had to be given to actual rather than formal relations, to real intelligible rather than logical relations.

There is no doubt that Philoponos employed sharp logical arguments when analyzing and criticizing the arguments of his opponents, not least in his refutation of Aristotle's scientific theories as in his exposure of the inconsistencies in his static theory of light. However, in giving a positive account of light in accordance with its dynamic nature, he deployed a dynamical and holistic approach. Simplicius accused Philoponos of being woefully ignorant of logic and of having no knowledge of syllogisms! What Simplicius did not realize was that there is not and cannot be any logical relation between ideas and realities, far less between ideas and dynamical realities. By their very nature real intelligible relations cannot be cast into an abstract or logical forms of thought. Like Clerk Maxwell more than a thousand years later he had to make use of something like physical or dynamical reasoning, and operate with what has been called a material logic (*Sachlogik*) rather than a formal logic (*Sprachlogik*). Thus it my well be said that in his dynamic scientific thinking Philoponos anticipated something of the epistemological revolution in Einstein's general relativity theory as to the way in which empirical and rational factors are interrelated and bear upon one another at every level of reality and our scientific explanations, not to speak of the fact that logic, like Euclidean geometry, applies only to flat space and not space-time.

We must now ask how this dynamic and relational way of thinking in his science, strictly in accordance with the nature or reality of things, affected Philoponos' *theology* in giving it a dynamic form in the doctrine of God and of salvation. The crunch came over the precise meaning that had now to be given to the Greek terms for nature, being, hypostasis and person (φύσις, οὐσία, ὑπόστασις, πρόσωπον), which had already been stretched, changed, and developed under the dynamic impact of the Gospel. In that event attention had to be given to their *actual use* in God's saving activity rather than to their classical dictionary definitions. That change was accentuated by Philoponos' dynamic and relational thinking. While the dynamic theology of the great Alexandrian theologians had influenced his science, his own powerful dynamic science was now to influence his theology. As his theology had effected a dynamic change in his science, so his science deepened the dynamic understanding of God and his saving activity. In God divine being and divine act are one, μία οὐσία and μία ἐνέργεια are perfectly one. He is the mighty living acting God whose being and act are, so to speak, the obverse of one another. The reciprocal relation between God's being and God's activity was nowhere more evident than in Philoponos' use of the expression μία φύσις or one nature to speak of the μία ἀλήθεια or the one reality of the incarnate Son of God. With Philoponos those Greek terms were now given a realist dynamic slant in line with his science: God *is* living and dynamic in his very nature. And so when he interpreted the Athanasian and Cyrilian expression "one incarnate nature (μία φύσις σεσαρκωμένη)" of Christ in a dynamic way to refer to him as the one incarnate reality of the Son of God, where the terms nature (φύσις) and reality (ἀλήθεια) were being used as scientific equivalents, as in Alexandrian dogmatic science (δογματικὴ ἐπιστήμη) in a way that was scientifically and theologically synonymous. He was not denying that Jesus Christ had a divine nature and a human nature in one Person (far from it as he made very clear in his theological work *Diaitetes*, or *Arbiter*, presented to the Emperor Justinian), but was insisting that as God and Man he was one incarnate Reality, and in no sense schizoid. However, his dynamic way of thinking theologically of the Incarnate nature and reality of the Son of God was not recognized by the Aristotelian Establishment in Byzantium, so that John Philoponos was condemned by them and then anathematized as a monophysite heretic (one who denied the two natures of Christ). That had the disastrous effect of condemning his writings and rejecting his revolution of natural science for many, many centuries. In fact it was not until the revolutionary change that started with the work of James Clerk Maxwell in his combination of light theory and impetus theory that our modern empirico-theoretical science actually arose. Some of Philoponos' works were recovered during the Renaissance, and it is interesting to note that two of his works which I have been using, *De opificio mundi*, and *In animam Aristotelis*, were in John Calvin's Genevan library! However, in spite of some renewed acquaintance with him, *European classical science buried the scientific advance of* John Philoponos! With Galileo (1564-1642) and Isaac Newton (1643-1727) Aristotle's concept of inertia, the dominance of Euclidean geometry and Aristotelian logic, gave rise to the kind of determinist and mechanistic thought that prevailed until James Clerk Maxwell.

How then is John Philoponos now regarded? Under pressure from some of us, Professor George Dragas and myself, the anathema against Philoponos has now been lifted by the Greek Orthodox Church, but not yet by the Roman Catholic Church, due to the massive hang-over of Aristotelian thought in its philosophical and theological tradition. (Cf. TFT: 1990, *John Paul II on Science and Religion, Reflections from New View from Rome,* Vatican, 1990, pp 105-112.)

2. *James Clerk Maxwell*

James Clerk Maxwell was an evangelical and ecumenical believer, brought up by a Presbyterian father, who built Corsock Parish Church in Kirkcudbrightshire, Scotland, and an Episcopalian mother who taught him as a boy to believe that it was the God whom we know in Jesus Christ who created the world and gave it the life and beauty which he enjoyed in the Maxwell Glenlair estate in Galloway. Later on when the young Clerk Maxwell went to Edinburgh Academy and was taught Newtonian physics, he found it hard to believe that the God whom he knew in Jesus Christ had made the world in that kind of mechanistic way. What really interested him in physics was the embodiment of geometrical patterns and physical relations exhibited by nature particularly in its dynamic forms. Even as a schoolboy he wrote two accounts of how things might operate in a non-mechanistic and more dynamic way. They were judged so good that they were read by the Edinburgh Professor of Physics to the Royal Society of Edinburgh. It was typical of his devout belief in the Creator that when many years later he was appointed to the chair of Experimental Physics in Cambridge, he had carved on the door of the Cavendish Laboratory words from Psalm 111 in Latin, *Magna opera Domini exquisita in omnes voluntates ejus*: "The works of God are great, sought out of all them that have pleasure therein".

Like his father Clerk Maxwell was a devoted churchman and became a church elder in Corsock Kirk. Even when he lived in England, in London or Cambridge, he made a point of riding back to Corsock during the Communion season to prepare the parishioners committed to his charge for Holy Communion. It was undoubtedly his Christian commitment and deep evangelical faith, with a powerful `mystical' ingredient in his soul and an intuitive slant of mind, which prompted and guided him in working out the conceptual interrelation between his science and his Christian belief. It is ultimately to him that we owe the radical change in our understanding of physical reality and of the rational structure of physics, due to his discovery of the mathematical properties of light, moving at 186 thousand miles a second, and its unique status in the universe of space and time. In bringing his distinctive form of light theory and impetus theory together, to which he gave expression in his epoch-making work *A Dynamical Theory of the Electromagnetic Field*, he formulated his famous differential equations, and in his great work *A Treatise on Electricity and Magnetism*, he laid the foundations upon which our empirico-theoretical science rests, and supplied the platform for their further advance. That work must be reckoned with Newton's *Principia Mathematica* as one of the two great works on which all modern science rests.

My concern here, then, is not with Clerk Maxwell's theology as such, but with the fact that his theological grasp of divine truth opened his mind to a more realist understanding of the contingent nature of the world and its distinctive rational order, and exercised a creative and regulative role in the choice and formation of scientific concepts and theories and their explanatory development. It was his concept of the continuous dynamic field that Einstein hailed as the greatest change in the rational structure of science. It is not surprising; therefore, that Albert Einstein kept a portrait of James Clerk Maxwell in his study at the Institute of Advanced Studies in Princeton. What lay behind that great change, however, which Einstein did not realize, was Clerk Maxwell's adaptation to physics of the *relational way of thinking* which in Scotland went back through Sir William Hamilton, whose classes in metaphysics in Edinburgh Clerk Maxwell attended as a student, ultimately to John Duns Scotus. In his early work Clerk Maxwell, in line with the dominant Newtonian tradition, made several attempts to offer a mechanistic explanation of the electro-magnetic field put forward by Michael Faraday, but he remained dissatisfied. In his understanding of the nature of the created order, he could not believe that the modes of connection in nature were of a mechanical kind. And so instead he offered a very different dynamic and relational interpretation.

The revolution in physics advanced by Clerk Maxwell's dynamical theory was too deep and strange for his scientific friends. Lord Kelvin even charged Clerk Maxwell with lapsing into "mysticism", when he abandoned his mechanical model. It was on the same ground that Clerk Maxwell attacked the molecular determination of Continental physicists in the nineteenth century - and now the twentieth century is still struggling to fall into line! Lord Kelvin was certainly a Christian believer, and a faithful member of the Church of Scotland, but he lacked the kind of deep intuitive insight that Clerk Maxwell gained through the evangelical teaching of his mother and father about the creation and incarnation. Clerk Maxwell did not intrude theological ideas specifically or directly into his scientific theories, but the Christian faith deeply entrenched in his being exercised a very significant role in his choice and formation of his leading scientific concepts. Thus through his "union with Christ", of which he spoke frequently, he gained an intuitive apprehension of the relation of God to his creation, which provided him with what he called "a fiducial point or standard of reference" for discriminating scientific judgments. It directed him to real ends external to himself, and to the kind of objectivity he needed for critical scientific activity, not least his grasping and bringing to appropriate expression the kind of contingent intelligible relations inherent in nature. This called for a holistic rather than an abstractive way of thinking, and a holistic mode of reasoning, in which he could let real dynamic relations have their full value, without being mauled by abstract Aristotelian logic or flattened by Euclidean geometric patterns which do not apply to dynamic space-time relations and structures. Hence he inverted the current mathematical and scientific way of beginning with analytical particulars and building up the whole by synthesis, and made primary a mathematico-conceptual mode of interpreting dynamic realities and real ontological intelligible relations without distorting them. At the same time his Christian faith provided

Clerk Maxwell with certain "analogical truths", root ideas, and fundamental conceptions, for which natural science could not account but which guided him in the scientific task of wedding thought with objective realities and developing appropriate ideas for their interpretation. He spoke of these as "modes of thought" and "physical truths" matched to the unveiling of processes inherent in nature, which called for an "embodied mathematics", a corresponding mode of what he called "physical and dynamical reasoning" together with a "new mathesis in mathematics" particularly concerned with dynamic ontological relations of space and time. In that connection he called for a new way of mathematical thinking involving time relations, which was later echoed by Einstein, but which no one has yet been able to achieve.

Clerk Maxwell became convinced that "in a scientific point of view *relation is the most important thing to know*". The kind of relations he wanted to express and develop were not of a putative kind but real relations of an ontological kind inhering in reality, for the inter-relations of things are ontologically constitutive of what they really are. The relations between things even of persons belong to what they are. That was a conviction deeply embedded in Scottish theology, particularly in the thinking of what Clerk Maxwell called "the old divines" in which the notion of person was held to be controlled by the person-constituting and person-intensifying activity of God in the Incarnation, such that union with Christ becomes the ground for inter-personal relations in the Church. Relations between persons have ontological force and are part of what persons are as persons - they are real, person-constituting relations. That was the theology underlying Clerk Maxwell's concept of union with Christ and of inter-personal relations in Christ, which it was not his nature to isolate in some compartmentalized way from his understanding of real, ontological relations in the physical universe.

Of special significance for him was, I believe, the teaching by Robert Boyd of Trochrig on the Holy Trinity, in his great work *Praelectiones in Ephesios*. In it Boyd expounded the Patristic conception of the *anhypostasis* and *enhypostasis* of the incarnate being of Christ as God and man in one Person, in which he anticipated Karl Barth! But he also explained the perichoretic inter-relations between the Persons of the Holy Trinity who are what they are in their subsistent hypostatic relations with one another. On that analogy he showed that on a human level the relations between persons belong substantially not accidentally to what they really are. Relation there is the most important thing to know. That is the kind of ontological and dynamical relation which Clerk Maxwell was to call to his aid when again and again he failed to offer a satisfactory explanation of the behavior of the moving lines of force in the electromagnetic field in terms of Newtonian physics and mechanics. Relation understood in this ontological and dynamical way is a primary instance of what Clerk Maxwell called "analogical truths", root ideas and fundamental conceptions for which natural science could not account but which guided him in the scientific task of wedding thought with reality and developing appropriate ideas. He spoke of these as "modes of thought" and "physical truths" matched to the unveiling of processes inherent in nature, which called for a corresponding mode of "physical reasoning", of "embodied mathematics", and in fact for "new mathesis in mathematics" particularly concerned with the dynamic and ontological relations of space and time. Thus when Clerk Maxwell put forward an explanation of the behavior of electromagnetic particles which are what they are in onto-dynamical relation to one another, in particular of the way in which the particles of light moving at the speed of light relate ontologically to one another, he came up with the concept of the *continuous dynamic field*, and developed equations which are laws representing the structure of the field. The formulation of those equations Einstein held to be the most important event in physics since Newton's time. Clerk Maxwell's concept of the reality of the dynamical field had the effect of transforming the laws of classical Newtonian mechanics, and opened the way ahead toward a new understanding of physical reality in terms of relativity and quantum theory. It was a revolutionary counterpart to the transformation of Aristotelian science by John Philoponos in the sixth century through his combination of light theory and impetus theory. It was not that Clerk Maxwell imported theological conceptions as such into his science, but that it was the slant of his deeply Christian mind informed by faith that exercised a guiding role in the choice and formation of his leading scientific concepts. In was in fact the pressure of his Christian understanding of God made known through the Incarnation of his Word in Jesus Christ and of his creation of the world of space and time, that led him to adopt what he called holistic ways of thinking and to put forward new fundamental ideas that transformed the basic structure of natural science. That is to say, it was Clerk Maxwell's theological convictions that played a heuristic and effective role in the development of his science.

What about the relation of *light* to *word*, created light to the uncreated light of the Word of God, the transcendent source of all contingent rational order in the universe? We recall that it is to Clerk Maxwell that we owe the discovery that light has mathematical properties. Everything we know in the created universe, macrocosmically or microcosmically, we learn from light signals, but their mathematical patterns have to be deciphered and coordinated with word in the formulation of scientific theory and the development of knowledge. That is to say, as Philoponos had shown, in his distinction between uncreated Light and created light, that physical light was to be understood not merely through its empirical behavior, but through the bearing upon it of information which shaped its theoretical content - that is how he made his revolutionary discoveries. Expressed otherwise, it was through a "meta-relation" of light to "word", and above all to the uncreated Light and creative Word of God, that it came to be understood and deployed by Philoponos in his transformation of science. It was, as we have seen, through the cognitive content of his faith grounded in the revealed Word of God that Philoponos actually developed his epoch-making light theory and impetus theory. This raises for us the importance of what we call "information theory", and the need to take into account some sort of transcendent order, or "meta-plan" (as Paul Davies calls it), in developing scientific theory especially at the boundaries between being and non-being. That is, of course, particularly evident today in respect of the human genome which is laden with more information than would fill a vast encyclopedia, which by its astonishing complex nature could not have arisen in some sort of accidental or self-organisational way.

I believe that information is needed in the understanding of the behavior of physical light and its divinely given dynamic role in the universe. Created light by its very nature points away to the uncreated Light and Word of God, the ultimate ground of all rational order and the transcendent source of the crucial information needed in heuristic processes of science. John Philoponos and Clerk Maxwell together thus point us in seeking understanding of the universe toward some meta-source of knowledge or meta-order to guide our research and develop appropriate scientific theory that is to knowledge which we cannot gain through the inquiries of natural science alone. Natural processes by themselves cannot explain or generate order - what is needed is an intelligible in-put beyond them. Thus natural law by its very contingent nature points beyond itself to a transcendent ground of intelligibility in God, that is to what Einstein called the *Why* or ultimate reason and justification for the laws of nature. It is, I believe, along these lines that we may profitably think out for our generation the cognitive bearing of Christian belief upon the advance of scientific knowledge of the universe that God has made and within which his Word by whom all things are made became incarnate in space and time.

I believe then that, when we explore the way in which the Christian faith of John Philoponos in the sixth century and of James Clerk Maxwell in the nineteenth century exercised a cognitive input and creative impact upon natural science, we may discern something of the way in which we today, working at the conceptual interface between theological science and natural science, may contribute to genuine advance in scientific knowledge. But in so doing it will have a powerful feed-back upon Christian theology of the dynamic kind that it needs today, and a recovery of what Karl Barth has called the God who acts in freedom, the God whose Being and Act are dynamically one and the same.

Chapter 2

Einstein and God

In a recent book Max Jammer, Rector Emeritus of Bar Lan University in Jerusalem, a former colleague of Albert Einstein at Princeton, claims that Einstein's understanding of physics and his understanding of religion were profoundly bound together, for it seemed to Einstein that nature exhibited traces of God quite like "a natural theology". Indeed it is with the help of natural science that the thoughts of God may be tapped and grasped.[1] He spoke of God so frequently in this way that Friedrich Dürrenmatt once said "Einstein used to speak of God so often that I almost looked upon him as a disguised theologian".[2] I do not believe these references to "God" can be dismissed simply as a *façon de parler*, for God had a deep, if rather elusive, significance for Einstein which was not unimportant for his life and scientific activity. It indicated a deep-seated way of life and thought: "God" was not a theological mode of thought but rather the expression of a "lived faith" (*eines gelebten Glaubens*).

Albert Einstein was born in 1879 of secular Jewish parents who lived in Ulm and then in München, where he went to school. There in accordance with State law he had to be instructed in his faith, and was taught Judaism because of his ethnic heritage. By the age of twelve Einstein became deeply religious, combining ardent belief in God with a passion for the music of Mozart and Beethoven, and composed songs to the glory of God which he sang aloud to himself on his way to and back from school. Einstein regularly read the Bible, Old and New Testaments alike (which he continued to do throughout his life). He was taught the rudiments of Hebrew, but never mastered it, and avoided the course for the traditional Bar-Mitzwa. He reveled in mathematics and music, especially in playing the violin, but recoiled from rigid orthodox rites such as those regarding kosher food,[3] compulsory rules, and Talmudic ways of thought, and began to

---

[1]   Max Jammer, *Einstein und Die Religion*, Konstantz, 1995.

[2]   Friedrich Dürrenmatt, *Albert Einstein*, Zürich, 1979, p. 12, cited by Max Jammer, op. cit. p. 54: "Einstein pflegte so oft von Gott zu sprechen, dass ich beinahe vermute, er sei ein verkappter Theologe gewesen."

[3]   While in his religious years he tried to dissuade his parents from eating pork, it is related of a later occasion that when he and some friends were entering a restaurant, an Orthodox Jew asked whether the food was strictly kosher - Einstein replied, "Only

develop a distrust of all authority, including biblical and religious authority. He had an unusually independent attitude of mind, critical but not skeptical, which was accentuated by his resentment against the authoritarian discipline of his German schoolmasters. This led him to give up his uncritical religious fervor in order to liberate himself from what he spoke of as "the only personal", but without becoming atheistic or hostile to religion. He never lost his admiration for the fundamental ends and aspirations of the "Jewish-Christian religious tradition", and had no doubt of the significance of what he called those "superpersonal objects and goals which neither require nor are capable of rational foundation".[4] It was in this independent spirit, as "a typical loner", as he spoke of himself, without personal religious commitment, but with deep religious awe, that he cultivated and retained throughout his life unabated wonder at the immensity, unity, rational harmony, and mathematical beauty of the universe.

Later in life in a speech delivered in Berlin, he gave this illuminating account of himself.

"Although I am a typical loner in daily life, my consciousness of belonging to the invisible community of those who strive for truth, beauty, and justice has preserved me from feeling isolated. The most beautiful and deepest experience a man can have is the sense of the mysterious. It is the underlying principle of religion as well as all serious endeavor in art and science. He who never had this experience seems to me, if not dead, then at least blind. To sense that behind anything that can be experienced there is something that our mind cannot grasp and whose beauty and sublimity reaches us only indirectly and as a feeble reflection, this is religiousness. In this sense I am religious. To me it suffices to wonder at these secrets and to attempt humbly to grasp with my mind a mere image of the lofty structure of all that is there."[5]

Before Albert was sixteen when he would have been obliged to undertake military training, he decided to move from school, leave Germany, give up German citizenship, and join his parents who had moved to Italy. Instead of continuing his education in Italy, however, Einstein chose to attend a school in Aarau in Switzerland where he enjoyed a rather freer mode of study and continued to cultivate his passion for Mozart and physics and think out things in his own way. As he was not an ethnic Swiss he was exempted from military training, which gave him time to indulge in extra-curricular pursuits, such as natural history expeditions with friends. He taught himself calculus and kept musing and thinking about light: "wondering especially what things might look

---

an ox eats strictly kosher"! Denis Brian, *Einstein, a life*, New York 996, p.128. But Einstein was never disrespectful of the beliefs and habits of his orthodox friends.

[4]   Cf. Abraham Pais, `Subtle is the Lord...', Oxford, 1982, p. 319. Cf. also Einstein, *Ideas and Opinions*, New York,1954; "The highest principles for our aspirations and judgments are given to us in the Jewish-Christian religious tradition." See also Max Jammer, *op.cit.* p. 48f.

[5]   Cited by Denis Brian, *Einstein, a life*, New York, 1996, p. 234.

like if someone went along for the ride with a light wave, keeping pace with it as it traveled through space".[6] It was when he was 17 that he finally announced his exit from the Jewish Religious Fellowship. After Aarau Einstein went to Zürich where he took courses in electrical engineering at its world famous Polytechnic where one of his teachers was Hermann Minkowski, who in 1907 was to put forward the idea of four-dimensional space-time as an independent reality. Einstein's studies at Zürich led eventually to Einstein's first employment in a technical school at Wintertur, and then at the Swiss Patent Office in Bern, where he wrote his early epoch-making scientific papers published in *Annalen der Physik* for 1905.

Particularly interesting for our understanding of what Einstein held about God was his marriage to Mileva Maric, whom he had met in the physics classes, who belonged to a Greek Orthodox family in Serbia. While it was not personal belief or religious faith but physics which brought them together, there can be little doubt that it left some imprint on what he was to think and say of God, evident in the use he frequently made of terms such as "transcendent" and "incarnate" to speak of "the cosmic intelligence" which lay behind the universe of space and time, which seems to indicate that there was rather more than just a way of speaking in what he said and thought of God. This is clearly reflected in an interview which Einstein later in life gave to an American magazine *The Saturday Evening Post*, in 1929.

"To what extent are you influenced by Christianity?"

"As a child I received instruction both in the Bible and in the Talmud. I am a Jew, but I am enthralled by the luminous figure of the Nazarene."

"Have you read Emil Ludwig's book on Jesus?"

"Emil Ludwig's Jesus is shallow. Jesus is too colossal for the pen of phrasemongers, however artful. No man can dispose of Christianity with a *bon mot*."

"You accept the historical Jesus?"

"Unquestionably! No one can read the Gospels without feeling the actual presence of Jesus. His personality pulsates in every word. No myth is filled with such life."[7]

In view of this interview it is understandable that Einstein is reported to have said that Christ Jesus was the greatest of all Jews. Be that as it may, Einstein remained generally committed to the Jewish tradition and outlook, a commitment which became more and more resolute in face of Nazi attacks on himself and his Jewish scientific friends in Berlin, where he was appointed a Professor in 1913. The following year his wife Mileva with his two sons joined him in Berlin, but returned almost immediately to Switzerland - she hated Germany. Einstein wept when she left him - they were reluctantly divorced. He had once written to her, "You are and will remain a shrine for me to which no one has access." Several

---

[6]   See Denis Brian, *Einstein, a life*, New York, 1996, p. 12.

[7]   George Sylvester Viereck, "What Life Means to Einstein", *The Saturday Evening Post*, 26 October 1929.

years later he married a cousin, Elsa Löwenthal a widow in Berlin, who with her daughter Margot cherished him throughout the rest of his life. He continued to pursue his scientific research and teaching in Berlin, in spite of the Nazi campaign against the Universities, and the vilification of Einstein's special and general theory of relativity, especially after his publication of *Die Grundlage der allgemeinen Relativitätstheorie* in *Annalen der Physik* in 1916. In Einstein's fearless championing of academic freedom, which finally drove him and Michael Polanyi, his Jewish colleague in Berlin, abroad, Einstein went to Princeton and Polanyi went to Manchester. Throughout his years in Berlin he had retained the admiration and support of Max von Laue and Max Planck, but objections to nominations for the award of the Nobel Prize to Einstein were lodged year after year, in fact six times, by several leading German physicists, notably by the virulently anti-Semitic Nobel Laureate Philip Lenard. The award was finally made in 1922, for his work, not on relativity, but on the photoelectric effect - Einstein sent the prize money to Mileva.

The bitter persecution of the Jews in Germany had the effect of drawing Einstein into closer relations also with Christian people, as his personal friendships with Max and Heidi Born who had become Quakers in Edinburgh, and with the Ross Stevensons and Blackwoods of Princeton Theological Seminary, make clear. When the Rev. Andrew Blackwood handed him a magazine clipping about the interview published in the *Saturday Evening Post*, and asked him if it was accurate, he read it carefully and answered, "That is what I believe".[8]

While the hounding and harrowing slaughter of Jews in Germany, and attacks on him by anti-Semitic Americans, had the effect of making Einstein more and more resolute in open affirmation of his Jewishness, deepening the bond with his fellow Jews, they also had the effect of deepening his appreciation of the Christian Church and its opposition to Hitler and the holocaust. Here is a paragraph from a letter Einstein once sent to an American Episcopal Bishop about the behavior of the Church during the holocaust.

"Being a lover of freedom...I looked to the universities to defend it, knowing that they had always boasted of their devotion to the cause of truth; but, no, the universities immediately were silenced. Then I looked to the great editors of the newspapers whose flaming editorials in days gone by had proclaimed their love of freedom, but they, like the universities, were silenced in a few short weeks. Only the church stood squarely across the path of Hitler's campaign for suppressing the truth. I never had any special interest in the church before, but now I feel a great affection and admiration because the church alone has had the courage and persistence to stand for intellectual truth and moral freedom. I am forced to confess that what I once despised I now praise unreservedly"[9]

---

[8]   Denis Brian, *Einstein, a life*, New York, 1996, p. 277f.

[9]   Reported in *The Evening News*, Baltimore, April 13, 1979.

Let me relate here what a friend of mine in Princeton told me about an illuminating event one day during the war, when Einstein learned of a prayer-meeting where Christians gathered to make intercession for Jews in Germany. To their surprise Einstein came along from his home at 112 Mercer Street with his violin and asked if he might join them. They welcomed him warmly, and he `prayed' with his violin. Yet in relation to petitionary prayer Einstein not infrequently reacted against "the fact that men appeal to the Divine Being in prayers and plead for the fulfillment of their wishes", for that implied for him, as we will note, a selfish "anthropomorphic" idea of God which he rejected.[10]

I associate that incident in Princeton, when he joined a prayer meeting with his violin, with another event which took place in 1929 in Berlin, told to me by Max Jammer in a recent letter. It was the occasion when Yehudi Menuhin, the great Jewish violinist, gave a recital at a concert on Beethoven, Bach and Brahms, by the Berlin Philharmonic Orchestra conducted by Bruno Walter. Einstein was so overwhelmed that he rushed across the stage into Menuhin's dressing room, and exclaimed, "*Jetzt weiss ich, dass es einen Gott im Himmel gibt*" - "Now I know that there is a God in heaven."[11]

What does all this tell us about Einstein the scientist and "God"? That is a matter which calls for a more considered thought than is usually given. And so, in the rest of this lecture I would like to address myself to two questions; 1) What did "God" mean for Einstein himself, and 2) What did "God" imply for his mathematical and physical science?

1) *What did "God" mean for Einstein?*

Early in his life Einstein came to refer to God as "cosmic intelligence" which he did not think of in a personal but in a "super-personal" way, for, as he learned from Spinoza, the term "personal" when applied to human beings cannot *as such* be applied to God.[12] Nevertheless he resorted to the Jewish-Christian way of speaking of God who *reveals* himself in an ineffable way as truth which is its own certainty. Spinoza held that "truth is its own standard". "Truth is the criterion of itself and of the false, as light reveals itself and darkness," so that "he who has a true idea, simultaneously knows that he has a true idea, and cannot 778doubt concerning the truth of the thing perceived."[13] Hence once a thing is

---

[10]   See his 1939 address to Princeton Theological Seminary, *Ideas and Opinions*, New York, 1954, p.46.

[11]   This is also recounted by Denis Brian, *op. cit.*, p. 193.

[12]   Cf. Stuart Hampshire, *Spinoza*, revised edition, Harmondsworth, 1962, p. 49: "It is a general principle in Spinoza's philosophy, which he constantly repeats to prevent misunderstandings, that no term when applied to God can possibly bear the meaning which it has when applied to human beings."

[13]   Spinoza, *The Chief Works of Benedict De Spinoza*, Vol. II, *Ethica*, Proposition XLIII, tr. & edit. by R.H.M. Elwes, London, 1889, p. 114; *De Intellectus Emendatione*, pp. 12-19. Cf. Stuart Hampshire, *Spinoza*, p. 99f.

understood it goes on manifesting itself in the power of its own truth without having to provide for further proof.[14] Thus when God reveals himself to our minds, our understanding of him is carried forward by the intrinsic force of his truth as it continually impinges on our minds and presses for fuller realization within them. It was in this kind of way that Einstein thought of God as revealing himself in the wonderful harmony and rational beauty of the universe, which calls for a mode of non-conceptual intuitive response in humility, wonder and awe which he associated with science and art. It was particularly in relation to science itself, however, that Einstein felt and cultivated that sense of wonder and awe. Once when Ernest Gordon, Dean of Princeton University Chapel, was asked by a fellow Scot, the photographer Alan Richards, how he could explain Einstein's combination of great intellect with apparent simplicity, he said, "I think it was his sense of reverence."[15] That was very true: Einstein's religious and scientific instincts were one and the same, for behind both it was his reverent intuition for God, his unabated awe at the thoughts of "the Old One", that was predominant. Although Einstein was not himself a committed Jewish believer he would certainly have agreed with the call of Rabbi Shmuel Boteach today to restore *God* himself, rather than *halacha*, as the epicentre of Judaism.[16]

> "Science can only be created", Einstein said, "by those who are thoroughly imbued with the aspiration toward truth and understanding. This source of feeling, however, springs from the sphere of religion. To this there also belongs the faith in the possibility that the regulations valid for the world of existence are rational, that is, comprehensible to reason. I cannot conceive of a genuine scientist without that profound faith. The situation may be expressed by an image: science without religion is lame, religion without science is blind."[17]

That statement comes from his 1939 address to Princeton Theological Seminary, but far from being unique, it is reflected in statement after statement he made about science, religion, and God.

When Count Kessler once said to him, "Professor! I hear that you are deeply religious." Calmly and with great dignity, Einstein replied, "Yes, you can call it that. Try and penetrate with our limited means the secrets of nature and you will find that, behind all the discernible concatenations, there remains something subtle, intangible and inexplicable. Veneration for this force beyond anything that we can comprehend is my religion. To that extent I am, in point of fact, religious."[18] Einstein was certainly no positivist.

Here are some other statements Einstein made about this:

---

[14]   *Tractatus de intellectus emendatione*, edit. by R. H. M. Elwes, p. 19.

[15]   Alan Windsor Richards, *Einstein as I Knew Him,* Princeton, 1979.

[16]   Rabbi Shmuel Boteach, *The Jewish Chronicle*, 26.10.96.

[17]   *Ideas and Opinions*, New York, 1954, p. 46.

[18]   Cited by Denis Brian, *op. cit.* p. 161.

"By way of the understanding he [the scientist] achieves a far-reaching emancipation from the shackles of personal hopes and desires, and thereby attains that humble attitude of mind towards the grandeur of reason incarnate in existence, and which, in its profoundest depths, is inaccessible to man. This attitude, however, appears to me to be religious, in the highest sense of the word. And so it seems to me that science not only purifies the religious impulse of the dross of its anthropomorphism but also contributes to a religious spiritualization of our understanding of life."[19]

"My religion consists of a humble admiration of the illimitable superior Spirit who reveals himself in the slight details we are able to perceive with our frail and feeble minds. The deeply emotional conviction of the presence of a superior reasoning Power, which is revealed in the incomprehensible universe, forms my idea of God."[20]

Yet again:

"You will hardly find one among the profounder sort of scientific minds without a peculiar religious feeling of his own...His religious feeling takes the form of a rapturous amazement at the harmony of natural law, which reveals an intelligence of such superiority that, compared with it, all the systematic thinking and acting of human beings is an utterly insignificant reflection."[21]

Still again, in another version of this statement, Einstein said:

"Certain it is that a conviction, akin to religious feeling, of the rationality and intelligibility of the world lies behind all scientific work of a higher order. The firm belief, which is bound up with deep feeling, in a superior mind revealing himself in the world of experience, represents my conception of God, which may, therefore be described in common parlance as `pantheistic' (Spinoza)".[22]

What did Einstein mean, then, when he referred to God as "cosmic intelligence", "the grandeur of reason incarnate in existence", to which he not

---

[19]   *Out of My Later Years*, New York, 1950, p. 32; and *Ideas And Opinions*, New York, 1954, p. 49.

[20]   Cited by Lincoln Barnett, *The Universe and Einstein*, New York, 1948, Mentor soft cover edition, 1963, p. 109.

[21]   *Ideas and Opinions*, New York, 1954, p. 40.

[22]   Einstein, *The World as I See It*, London, 1955, p. 131.

infrequently referred in a Talmudic expression as "the Old One"? He was not always consistent so that it is not easy to grasp precisely what he meant. But it seems clear that he conceived of God as the ultimate spiritual ground of all rational order which transcends what the scientist works with as natural laws - a point to which we shall return later - but unlike the Jewish-Christian religion he did not think of that in what he called a "personal" or "anthropomorphic" way, that is, as a God conceived in man's image, but in a "superpersonal" (*ausserpersönlichen*) way freed from the fetters of the "only personal" (*Nur-Persönlichen*), or people's selfish desires.

"What is important", he said, "is the force of this superpersonal content and depth of the conviction concerning its overpowering meaningfulness, regardless of whether an attempt is made to unite this content with the divine Being for otherwise it would not be possible to count Buddha and Spinoza as religious personalities. Accordingly, a religious person is devout in the sense that he has no doubt of the significance and loftiness of these superpersonal objects and goals which neither require nor are capable of rational foundation."[23]

Einstein was often asked "Do you believe in God?", to which he sometimes replied "I believe in Spinoza's God, who reveals himself in the harmony of all being".[24] "By God", Spinoza wrote at the very beginning of his *Ethica*, "I mean a being absolutely infinite - that is, a substance consisting in infinite attributes, of which each expresses eternal and infinite essentiality". Proposition XV of *Ethica* stated: "Whatever is, is in God, and without God nothing can be, or be conceived."[25] Einstein certainly held, as his constant appeal to God showed, that without God nothing can be known, but what did he really mean by his appeal to Spinoza? Once in answer to the question "Do you believe in the God of Spinoza?" Einstein replied as follows.

> "I can't answer with a simple yes or no. I'm not an atheist and I don't think I can call myself a pantheist. We are in the position of a little child entering a huge library filled with books in many different languages. The child knows someone must have written those books. It does not know how. The child dimly suspects a mysterious order in the arrangement of the books but doesn't know what it is. That, it seems to me, is the attitude of even the most intelligent human being toward God. We see a universe marvelously arranged and obeying certain laws, but only dimly understand these laws. Our limited minds cannot grasp the mysterious force that moves the constellations. I am fascinated by

---

[23] *Ideas and Opinions*, p. 44f. In his reference to Buddha Einstein may have had Ben Gurion in mind or even David Bohm! Cf. the discussion, reported by Max Jammer, which Einstein once had with Rabindranath Tagore about his book "The Religion of Man", when Einstein said: "I am more religious than you are!" Op. cit. p. 43.

[24] See Denis Brian, *op.cit.* p. 127.

[25] See the translation by R.H.M. Elwes, London, 1889, pp. 45 & 51.

Spinoza's pantheism, but admire even more his contributions to modern thought because he is the first philosopher to deal with the soul and the body as one, not two separate things."[26]

In a letter to Henry Oldenburg, the secretary of the Royal Society, Spinoza declared, "I do not think it necessary for salvation to know Christ according to the flesh: but with the Eternal Son of God, that is the Eternal Wisdom of God, which had manifested itself in all things, and especially in the human mind, and above all in Christ Jesus, the case is far otherwise."[27] He himself, he claimed, "paid homage to the Books of the Bible, rather than to the Word of God."[28] Spinoza read the New Testament Scriptures as well as the Old Testament Scriptures, e.g. St John's Gospel and the Epistle to the Hebrews, in a Hebraic way. He complained to Henry Oldenburg: "You think that the texts in John's Gospel and in Hebrews are inconsistent with what I advance, because you measure oriental phrases by the standards of European speech; though John wrote his Gospel in Greek, he wrote it as a Hebrew."[29] That is what John Reuchlin used to call *veritas Hebraica*.[30] When another Jew, Martin Buber, whom Einstein had known for forty years, one day in Princeton pressed him hard to reveal his religious belief, Einstein said, "What we [physicists] strive for...is just to draw his lines after him." The deeper one penetrates into nature's secrets, he declared, the greater becomes one's respect for God.

Einstein held that the main source of the present-day conflicts between the spheres of religion and of science lay in "the concept of a personal God" for that was to think of God in an anthropomorphic way, and to project into him figurative images and human psychological notions of personality, which give rise, he held, to religious practices of worship and notions of providence shaped in accordance with human selfish desires. That did not mean that Einstein thought of God merely in some impersonal way, for, as we have noted, he thought of relation to God in a sublime *superpersonal* way which he confessed unable to grasp or express and before which he stood in unbounded awe and wonder. Hence he felt it deeply when Cardinal O'Connell of Boston charged him with being an atheist[31]. When a newspaperman once accosted him in California

---

26   Denis Brian, *op. cit.* p. 186.

27   Spinoza's *Correspondence*, letter LXXXIII - see *Spinoza's Works*, Vol. II, edit by R. H. M. Elwes, 1899, p. 299.

28   *A Theologico-Political Treatise, Spinoza's Works*, vol. I, p.9.

29   Letter XXIII (LXXV), *The Chief Works of Spinoza*, Vol. II, London, 1889, p. 303.

30   John Reuchlin, *De verbo mirifico*, 1552, 2.7, p. 129. Cf. my essay "The Hermeneutics of John Reuchlin, 1455-1522", *Church, Word and Spirit, Historical and Theological Essays in Honor of Geoffrey W. Bromiley*, Edited by J.E. Bradley & R.A. Muller, Grand Rapids, 1987, pp. 107-121.

31   Cf. Max Jammer, *op.cit.* p.54; and Helen Dukas, *Albert Einstein - The Human Side*, Princeton, 1979, p. 132.

with the question, "Doctor is there a God?", Einstein turned away with tears in his eyes.[32]

What, then, did Einstein mean by claiming to believe in Spinoza's *Amor Dei Intellectualis*, the intellectual love of God, the highest happiness that man can know? He was approving of Spinoza's idea that to be rational is to love God and to love God is to be rational, so that for one to engage in science is to think the thoughts of God after him. With Spinoza, however, that involved the outright identification of God with nature, a causally concatenated whole, whereas, as we have seen, with Einstein the *Verständlichkeit* of God was so exalted that it could not be reduced to the logico-causal intelligibilities of nature. A transcendent relation had to be taken into account. As a Jew himself Einstein naturally resonated with Spinoza, the greatest of all modern Jewish philosophers, for they shared in the traditional unitary concept of man as body of his soul and soul of his body. Although there was much in Spinoza's philosophy which Einstein could not accept, what did appeal to him was Spinoza's rejection of Cartesian and other forms of dualism, and his unitary conception of the universe with its inherent rational harmony. That was both a help and a problem for Einstein. It fuelled his great drive toward unified field-theory, and his rejection of a dualism between time and space, wave and particle, relativity theory and quantum theory, but Spinoza's logico-mathematical and hard causalist uniformity gave rise to an absolute rigid determinism which conflicted with Einstein's realist and dynamic understanding of the openness of the universe, in his rejection of the closed Euclidean system of the world.

Here let me refer to a very interesting letter, recorded by Helen Dukas, which Einstein wrote to a child who asked him whether scientists prayed. "I have tried to respond to your question as simply as I could. Here is my answer. Scientific research is based on the idea that everything that takes place is determined by laws of nature, and therefore this holds for the actions of people. For this reason, a research scientist will hardly be inclined to believe that events could be influenced by prayer, i.e. by a wish addressed to a supernatural Being. However, it must be admitted that our actual knowledge of these laws is only imperfect and fragmentary, so that, actually the belief in the existence of basic all-embracing laws in nature also rests on a sort of faith. All the same this faith has been largely justified so far by the success of scientific research. But, on the other hand, everyone who is seriously involved in the pursuit of science becomes convinced that a spirit is manifest in the laws of the Universe - a spirit vastly superior to that of man, and one in the face of which we with our modest powers must feel humble. In this way the pursuit of science leads to a religious feeling of a special sort, which is indeed quite different from the religiosity of someone more naive."[33]

---

[32] Denis Brian, *op.cit.* p. 206.

[33] *Albert Einstein: The Human Side*, edited by Helen Dukas and Banesh Hoffmann, Princeton University Press, 1989, p. 32f. My attention has been drawn to this passage by Mark Koonz, formerly of Princeton Theological Seminary.

This brings me to my second question.

2) *What did "God" imply for Einstein's mathematical and physical science?*

Early in his career Einstein's studies of Newton and Kepler convinced him that there is no logical path to knowledge of the laws of nature, for there is no logical bridge between phenomena and their theoretical principles.[34] This was greatly reinforced by his study of James Clerk Maxwell.[35] It is the extra-logical problem, he held, that is essential, namely, the ontological reference of thought to reality.[36] Within the preestablished harmony of the universe, "ideas come from God" - they are revealed to the mind tuned into the master plan of the universe, and are apprehended through intuition resting on sympathetic understanding of experience. "He [the scientist] has to persist in his helpless attitude towards the separate results of empirical research, until principles which he can make the basis of deductive reasoning have revealed themselves to him."[37] "The supreme task of the physicist is to arrive at those elementary universal laws from which the cosmos can be built up by deduction. There is no logical path to these laws; only intuition resting on sympathetic understanding of experience, can reach them...There is no logical bridge between phenomena and their theoretical principles; that is what Leibnitz described so happily as a `preestablished harmony.'"[38] Einstein used to speak of this non-logical, intuitive way of reaching knowledge, as "tapping into God's thoughts".[39] "The deeper one penetrated into nature's secrets, the greater becomes one's respect for God."[40] Once when drawing out the implications of relativity theory in an amusing way which he hoped was in tune with the thoughts of God, he said "I cannot possibly know whether the good Lord does not laugh at it and has led me up the garden path"!"[41] I think of that in connection with the fact that the equations of relativity theory predict their own limits, and thus direct us back to a zero point in the expansion of the universe from what is commonly known as "the black hole", which, as

---

[34] Einstein, *The World as I See It*, London, 1935, p. 125f.

[35] See *The Evolution of Physics, from Early Concepts to Relativity and Quanta*, by Albert Einstein and Leopold Infeld, New York, 1938, pp. 125ff; and "Maxwell's Influence on the Development of the Conception of Physical Reality", by Einstein, reproduced in my edition of James Clerk Maxwell, *A Dynamical Theory of the Electromagnetic Field*, Edinburgh, 1982, pp. 29-32.

[36] *Ibid.* p. 174.

[37] *Ibid.* p. 128; and see the Essay on "Physics and Reality", *Out of My Later Years*, New York, 1950, pp. 60ff.

[38] *The World as I See It*, p. 125f.

[39] Cf. Denis Brian, *op.cit.* pp. 61 & 173.

[40] Cited by Denis Brian, *op.cit.* p. 129.

[41] Cf. again Denis Brian, *op.cit.* p. 67.

Henry Margenau held, implied the principle of *creatio ex nihilo*.[42] Einstein pointed out that "one must not conclude that the beginning of the expansion of the universe] must mean a singularity in the mathematical sense." Then he added: "This consideration does, however, not alter the fact that the `beginning of the world' really constitutes a beginning."[43] Such a beginning, a *creatio ex nihilo*, was of course an idea which was ruled out by Spinoza's *Deus sive Natura* notion of God as an infinite, eternal self-creating substance, and of his conception of the universe as non-contingent and completely necessary in its identification with God.

Now in order to indicate something of what "God" meant for Einstein's science, let us consider the bearing of three of his often repeated epigrammatic `sayings' about God: "God does not play dice"; "God does not wear his heart on his sleeve"; and "the Lord is subtle but not malicious."

(1) *"God does not play dice"*.

This seems to have been suggested by one of the propositions of Spinoza's *Ethics*, "In the nature of things nothing accidental is granted, but all things are determined by the necessity of the divine nature for existing and working in a certain way. In short, *there is nothing accidental in nature.*"[44] "God does not play dice" was asserted again and again by Einstein in connection with his belief in a fully rational world of law and order, and in rejection of the appeal to random elements in certain forms of quantum theory, e.g. the so-called "uncertainty principle" put forward by Heisenberg. Far from having explanatory value what is called *chance* is after all a negative way of thinking, or rather a way of not thinking. Einstein's "God" would not allow him to rest content with anything less than a rigorous scientific description of the intrinsic orderliness of nature at its micro-physical as well as at every other level of reality. Einstein once wrote of his objections to the then current form of quantum theory that his view of the matter "does not represent a blind-man's buff with the idea of reality".[45] "God does not play dice", imports a belief in an objective intelligibility in the continuous dynamic structures and transformations in the space-time reality of the universe which we may apprehend, but only at relatively elementary levels through open structures, even though they are mathematically precise in their formalization. As I understand him even Heisenberg toward the end of his life

---

[42]   Henry Margenau, *Thomas and the Physics of 1958*, Milwaukee, 1958, pp. 41 43. See Max Jammer, op.cit., pp. 102f. & 115.

[43]   A. Einstein, *The Meaning of Relativity*, Princeton, 1953, p. 129.

[44]   Baruch Spinoza, *Ethica*, proposition XXIX: *In rerum natura nullum datur contingens, sed omnia ex necessitate divinae naturae determinata sunt ad certo modo existendum et operandum*. Eng. Tr. by Andrew Boyle, Everyman's Library, vol. 481, London, 1959, p. 23. See also Max Jammer, *op.cit.* p. 38f.

[45]   Irene Born, *The Born-Einstein Correspondence*, London, 1971, p. 180f.

concluded that in quantum theory the scientist is in touch with nature which in its depth is so subtle and elusive that it cannot be explained in terms of the couplet "chance and necessity". That "God does not play dice" highlights the fact that *chance* is after all a negative way of thinking, or rather a way not to think. This is a lesson I believe that many scientists today, especially perhaps in biology, need to learn - their appeal to "chance" too often appears to be a sort of "scientist's God of the gaps"!

Behind all Einstein's thought lay the role given in the Jewish-Christian religion to the **primacy and constancy of light**. Recall the Genesis account of creation - the primacy of light: **"And God said, Let there by light: and there was light."** God is himself eternal *uncreated Light*, but he created the universe in such a way that it is governed by *created light*. We cannot see light, but see only what is lit up by light. We shall return to this later. It is through deciphering light signals that all our knowledge of the cosmos in macroscopic and microscopic levels is learned. We owe that to James Clerk Maxwell who discovered the mathematical properties of light, and the central role they have in scientific theory. Clerk Maxwell was followed by Einstein in giving light a primary place in his scientific description of the space/time universe. As Hermann Weyl, Einstein's colleague in Princeton, expressed Einstein's understanding of light: all bodies in motion are defined relationally in terms of space and time, and space and time are defined relationally with reference to light, but light is NOT defined with reference to anything else. Light has a unique physical and metaphysical status in the universe - it is an ultimate factor, the **Constant** expressed as **C** in scientific equations. (thus Einstein's famous formula, $E = MC^2$). If light were not constant, if the movement of light varied or wobbled in any way, there would be no order, only random disorderly events, chaos. It is light that reveals the orderly nature of things. That is why Einstein recoiled from giving random or chance-events a role in scientific explanation or the formulation of scientific theory.

The constancy of light throughout the created order reflects the **faithfulness** of God of which the Hebrew and Christian Scriptures all speak -God does not play dice. Yes, it was Einstein's belief in *God*, in God as the ultimate ground of all order, rational and moral order, which governed his scientific thinking and daily life. Spinoza, no less than Einstein, believed in the faithfulness of God - but the oneness he posited between God and nature meant for Spinoza that the kind of order he envisaged was of a determinist kind to be understood in terms of rigid logico-causal connections. Now there are clearly deep problems here in Einstein's appeal to the God of Spinoza. Like Spinoza he was right to reject a strict bifurcation of nature into mind and body, subject and object, but what of Spinoza's rigidly logical and causalist conception of God and the universe? In insisting that "God does not play dice", Einstein was accused, for example by Max Born, of being a hard-line determinist, but as Wolfgang Paula showed, writing to Born in Edinburgh from Princeton,[46] Einstein was not a determinist but a *realist*, with the conviction that, in line with Clerk Maxwellian field theory and

---

[46]   Irene Born, *The Born-Einstein Letters*, London, 1971, pp. 217-218 & 322-224.

general relativity theory, nature is governed by profound levels of intelligible connection that cannot be expressed in the crude terms of classical causality and traditional mathematics. He was convinced that the deeper forms of intelligibility being brought to light in relativity and quantum theory cannot be understood in terms of the classical notions of causality - they required what he called *Übercausalität* - supercausality. And this called for "an entirely new kind of mathematical thinking", not least in unified field theory - that was a kind of mathematics he did not even know, but which someone must find.[47]

(2) *"God does not wear his heart on his sleeve"*.

In their Jewish tradition both Einstein and Spinoza adhered strictly to the second Commandment that forbade thinking of God in any image or visible form. With Spinoza this was evidently reflected in his rejection of sense-perception as a mode of genuine objective knowledge. That is also the fundamental idea expressed in the statement "God does not wear his heart on his sleeve" which Einstein applied to physical science. It formulates the profound conviction that the real secrets of nature, its hidden intelligible order cannot be read off appearances, or be logically derived from the observational patterns of its phenomenal surface, but only by "tapping into the thoughts of God" as he "reveals" them to us. We cannot see God, but we may see him in the light of his own light. As the Hebrew Psalmist declared, "In thy light we see light."

Let us recall here the point noted earlier about the central light in the created universe. There we were concerned with the constancy of light, but here our concern is with the *invisibility* of light. It is through deciphering the mathematical patterns carried by light signals that all our knowledge of the space/time universe in its vast or tiny dimensions is derived. This understanding of light initiated an immense revolution in scientific inquiry, for it meant that the invisible is not to be explained in terms of the visible, but the visible in terms of the invisible. We do not see light itself, but see only what is lit up by light - "grasping reality in its depth", "tapping into the thoughts of the Old One", as Einstein used to say. "God does not wear his heart on his sleeve." This is not to say that Einstein was concerned to look for hidden causes detached from, or of a different category from, the ordered regularity we experience in our everyday world, for he was just as concerned to reject the `occult' as Bacon and Newton, and was even more concerned than they were, because he would have nothing to do with the kind of dualism upon which the occult seemed to thrive. Einstein's concern was rather to penetrate into the deep invisible dynamic ontological structure of the ordered regularity of things to which the phenomenal patterns of that regularity are coordinated, and by which they are controlled. That is particularly evident in the epistemological revolution brought about by general relativity theory which showed that empirical and theoretical factors, being and form, belong together at all levels of nature and our knowledge of it. Hence scientific inquiry must

---

[47] See the report of Denis Brian, *Einstein, A Life*, New York, 1996, p. 370.

penetrate into the inner imageless constitutive structure of things, which is invariant through all relativity for the human knower, and which can be grasped not through observational or phenomenological investigation but only by intellective penetration or intuitive insight. While the outward shape on the surface of existence remains observable and imageable, and is variant for every observer, the invisible imageless ontological structure remains constant and invariant for all observers. As such it provides the objective frame underlying the observable variations correlated with it, and therein constitutes the integrative force of their order on the phenomenal level, even of their surface connection with appearances.

To grasp nature like that intuitively and unitively in its objective depth and inherent relatedness, and in such as way as to do full justice to the differences and relativities of our observational experience without allowing them to disintegrate into pluralistic relativism, is what rigorous science is about. But it does mean that we have to think in a dimension of ontological depth in which the surface of things is coordinated with a deep invisible, intelligible structure, and thus think empirical and theoretical factors, phenomenal and noumenal levels of reality together, if we are really to reach knowledge of things in accordance with their distinctive nature and constitutive ground. "God does not wear his heart on his sleeve".

There is, however, a deep difference here between Einstein's thought and that of Spinoza. Spinoza's philosophy was in its way a Jewish form of the old Latin Stoic idea of *deus sive natura*, for according to him there is only one all-inclusive self-caused substance "God or nature" which he identified with the universe conceived as an infinite necessary whole and which is to be understood only in a logical-causal way - for him "God" was in no sense transcendent to the universe. In contrast Einstein's formulation of the principle that "God does not wear his heart on his sleeve", imports a profounder sense of the astonishing intelligibility (*Verständlichkeit*) of the universe and its incomprehensible transcendent ground in God. "The scientist", he said, "is activated by a wonder and awe before the mysterious comprehensibility of the universe which is yet finally beyond his grasp".[48] "In its profoundest depths it is inaccessible to man".[49] That is why, for Einstein, science without religion is lame.

(3) *"Subtle is the Lord, but malicious he is not."*

This saying, now engraved above a fireplace of the faculty lounge of the Mathematics Department in Princeton, is the translation of *Raffiniert ist der Herr Gott, aber boshaft is Er Nicht.*[50] By that Einstein said he meant "Nature hides her

---

[48]   Einstein, *Out of My Later Years*, pp. 30,60.

[49]   *Ideas and Opinions*, p. 49; cf. also p. 40.

[50]   Thus Denis Brian, *op.cit.* p. 127.

secret because of her essential loftiness, but not by means of ruse."[51] It was, like the other sayings, often repeated, not always in the same words. I prefer the stronger form: *Raffiniert is der Herr God, aber hinterlistig ist Er nicht*, which suggests that while God is subtle he is not wily or artful, he is deep but not devious - he does not deceive us or play tricks with us. If "God does not wear his heart on his sleeve" is meant to express the idea that the secrets of nature cannot be read off its phenomenal surface, "God is deep but not devious" expresses the complexity and subtlety yet ultimate simplicity and reliability of the universe. That is to say, the immanent order hidden behind the intricate and often baffling complex of connections which we find in the universe is essentially trustworthy, for in spite of all that might appear to the contrary when we come up against sets of events for which there seems to be no rational explanation, the universe is not arbitrary or evil, but unitary and trustworthy in its intelligibility.

This conviction relates to the point, to which I have referred earlier, that light has a unique physical and metaphysical status in the universe. If all bodies in motion are defined with reference to space and time, all space and time are defined with reference to light. Undefined by reference beyond itself, light is the great Constant, with reference to which all else we know in nature is relationally ordered, known and defined, and upon which we invariably rely. That holds good in spite of the fact that in our atomic and sub-atomic investigations, in terrestrial and astrophysical explorations of the universe as far as we can reach through space and time, we meet problems which may appear intractable to the laws of physics, as hitherto formalized. Throughout all the dynamic multivariable structures that pervade the universe of bodies in motion, somehow the constancy of light with its unique metaphysical status supports the conviction that "God does not play tricks with us". That is to say, there is an immanent order in the universe of the inviolability of which we remain totally convinced, for apart from it the universe would nowhere be accessible to rational inquiry and we ourselves who are creatures of space and time belonging to the universe could not be capable of rational thought or behavior of any kind. Thus while in the logical sense belief in order in the universe is neither verifiable nor falsifiable, it remains the most persistent of all scientific convictions, for without it there could be no science at all; hence we do not believe that there is or could be anything that can ultimately count against it. God is faithful, and does not let us down; he is always trustworthy.

That was a conviction to which Einstein remained very firmly committed in place of the claims of the quantum theorists who called in question the deep invariable order in the sub-atomic realm, where nature appeared to be causally discontinuous, and irrational. Einstein had himself to face a similar problem over the implications of general relativity for our understanding of a non-Euclidean universe of curved space, when he insisted that "as far as mathematical propositions refer to reality, they are not certain; and as far as they are certain

---

[51]   See Abraham Pais, `*Subtle is the Lord...*', Oxford, 1982, frontispiece.

they do not refer to reality."[52] Traditional logic applies to flat and not to curve space, so that new ways of thought are called for, which do not conform to the classical laws of logic and physics. That is why instead of going along entirely with the Copenhagen-Göttingen form of quantum theory, Einstein pointed to the need for "an entirely new kind of mathematics" to cope with the profound intelligible relations with which quantum scientists sought to grapple.[53] A profound revolution in the logical structure of science was needed, in line with and in development of the logical structure of science initiated by Clerk Maxwell, when he called for "a new mathesis" in mathematics, and pointed to the need for a dynamic kind of mathematics with time relations built into it. All this is to say, that in mathematical and scientific explanation a deeper more subtle way of thinking is needed, in which new factors of profound rationality have to be taken into account. God is subtle but not malicious or devious, and he does not lead us up the garden path, or ask us to play blind man's buff!

The way that Einstein so often connected the notion of *Order* with **God** reflects the fact that order is one of the ultimate beliefs which, while rational, cannot be proved - for we have to assume order either in trying to prove or disprove it - all rational order points beyond itself to an ultimate ground of order. That is why Einstein could not be an atheist, if only because apart from God the transcendent ground of all order, there could be no rational thought, let alone any science.

Now in concluding this lecture let me recall a point of great importance which few scientists today have taken up or perhaps dared to take into account. It is here that we can discern Einstein's sharpest deviation from the God of Spinoza. It was his adherence to Spinoza's rejection of dualism, and his insistence on the rational unity and lawful harmony of the universe, which made Einstein give so much attention for many years to the development of a unified field theory, one in which, for example, relativity theory and quantum theory could be united in a universal rational structure. Already in 1929 Einstein had raised a matter of great importance in this connection.[54] He pointed out that science has now reached the stage where it cannot be satisfied simply with describing *how* nature is what it is in its ongoing processes, but must press on to ask "*why* nature is what it is and not something else".[55] That is to say, science must not be satisfied with determining the laws of how nature as a matter of fact behaves, for if it wants to understand their "logical unity", to which he himself was committed in unified field theory, then science must penetrate into the transcendent ground of those

---

[52] "Geometry and Experience", the 1921 lecture to the Prussian Academy of Sciences, *Ideas and Opinions*, New York, 1954, p. 233.

[53] Refer to Denis Brian, *op.cit.* p. 370.

[54] "*Über den Gegenwärtigen Stand der Feld-Theorie*", *Festschrift zum 70. Geburtstag von Prof. Dr A. Stodola*, Zürich, 1929, pp. 126-132.

[55] Ibid., p. 126: "*Wir wollen nicht nur wissen wie de Natur is (und wie ihre Vorgänge ablaufen), sondern wir wollen...wissen warum die Natur so and nicht anders ist.*"

laws and find the ultimate justification for them. Einstein went on to say that this might appear to be a rather "Promethean" undertaking, but here we have to do with what he called "the religious basis of scientific enterprise."[56] To introduce the question *Why?* back into the inner structure of natural and physical science was to reject the rationalistic dualism of the Enlightenment between the *how* and the *why* to which are to be traced the damaging splits in western culture, but it was also to point to God as the ultimate ground of all rational order and the transcendent reason for all the laws of nature. What a startling light that throws upon what Einstein himself really meant by "God"! It is only from God that we can understand the **why** or the fundamental *purpose* of the created universe.

In view of this conviction, let me note two things. (1) Einstein never gave any attention to the problem of **evil** - evil is ultimately irrational and inexplicable, an abysmal mystery, as St Paul called it. There is *no reason why* to evil. (2) As far as I know, Einstein showed no interest in redemption - either in the biblical significance of atonement, or in the Jewish celebration of *Yom Kippur*. Yet it is only from God who does not play dice, who does not wear his heart on his sleeve, and who is deep but not devious, that we may be given an understanding of the ultimate reason for the created universe, and of his **redemptive purpose** for a world that has gone astray. It may be interesting to note that another Jewish scientist, Ilya Prigogine, who is not a believer, yet not a determinist like Spinoza who had no place in his thought for "time", has actually spoken of time as "redeemable".[57]

---

[56]   Einstein, Ibid., p. 127.

[57]   "The Rediscovery of Time", *Zygon, Journal of Religion & Science*, December, 1984, Vol. 19, No. 4, p. 444, with reference to T.S. Eliot, "Burnt Norton".

Chapter 3

Creation, Contingent World-Order, and Time: A Theologico-Scientific Approach

1

The concept of the creation of the universe out of nothing, *creatio ex nihilo*, originally derived from the Hebraic tradition, and became part of the Christian tradition from the beginning, but it was radicalized through the doctrine of the self-revelation of God in the incarnation and resurrection of his Son Jesus Christ. He was the divine Word or *Logos* by whom all things are made and through whom they are given temporal being in utter difference from God's eternal Being, and are endowed with a distinctive rationality dependent or contingent upon his transcendent rationality. The specific notion of *contingence* was developed by early Greek theology in order to express the nature of the universe as freely created in *matter and form* by God out of nothing, and endowed by him with an orderly reality of its own, utterly different from God yet dependent on him. By creation out of nothing was meant not created out of something called nothing, but not created out of anything. It was this Christian doctrine of the created universe and its contingent order that constituted the ultimate basis upon which all modern empirical science rests.

In line with this understanding of creation of the universe Christian thought rejected the prevailing dualist outlook of Greek science and philosophy, expressed in the sharp disjunction between the *cosmos noetos* and the *cosmos aisthetos*, or the *mundus intelligibilis* and the *mundus sensibilis*, as St Augustine spoke of it. That represented a far-reaching epistemological revolution, for it meant that the whole universe of invisible and visible or celestial and terrestrial realities was regarded, while creaturely and not divine, as permeated with a unitary rational order of a contingent kind, which could be investigated and understood only in accordance with its inherent nature, and not in accordance with any prior assumptions or logical reasoning from them. This gave rise to a strict understanding of knowledge, ἐπιστήμη, as the controlled understanding of things strictly in accordance with their divinely given or contingent nature, κατὰ φύσιν. In this way Christian thinkers broke new ground and put forward a new scientific method in showing how a conjunctive and synthetic mode of inquiry could penetrate into the nature of things and interpret them in accordance with their inner relations and intelligible structures. It will be sufficient for our purpose to refer only to thought of three leading Christian thinkers, Athanasius, Basil, and John Philoponos of Alexandria.

St Athanasius was convinced that when our minds act in obedience to the nature of created being, they are in tune with the rational order immanent in the created universe, and are already on the way of truth that leads to the really existent God. This does not mean that human beings can reach God by logical reasoning, but rather that through communing with the providential and regulating activity of God in the symmetry (συμμετρία), and order (τάξις), concord (ὁμόνοια), symphony (συμφωνία), and system (σύνταξις) of the cosmos, which point to the Creator, the human soul is directed to look away from creaturely rationalities to the uncreated and creative *Logos* of God. This is not some immanent reason in the universe, but the personal *Autologos* of the living and acting God who is other than created realities and all creation, the good Word of the good Father, who has established the order of all things, reconciling opposites into a single harmony. Thus Athanasius laid immense emphasis upon the one common order of the created cosmos, the intrinsic rationality of things, and so held that there is everywhere not finally chaos and disorder but one world order or harmonious system of the cosmos (κόσμου παναρμόνιος συντάξις) enlightened and regulated by the one creative *Logos*, in a sustained rejection of the dualism, pluralism and polymorphism of Hellenic philosophy, religion and science. The entire universe of visible and invisible, celestial and terrestrial, realities is a cosmic unity due to the all-embracing and integrating activity of the divine *Logos*, so that a single rational order pervades all created existence contingent upon the transcendent rationality of God. The universe created in this way he characterized as flowing or fleeting (ρευστός) in its temporality and as contingent (ἐνδεχόμενος) in its order.

It was in line with this changed outlook upon the universe that St Basil wrote his influential work, *Hexaemeron*, on the six "days" of creation, by which he did not mean calendar days but periods of unspecified duration, which reflected the biblical or Hebrew notion of `olam, the longest duration that can be conceived. Like the earlier Greek Fathers he spoke of time as created out of nothing along with the matter and form of the universe. He held that creation out of nothing means that there is an absolute origin to the universe, a transcendent beginning beyond all material and temporal beginning, which in the nature of the case we can know only by divine revelation. Basil argued that the created universe is *intrinsically incomplete* - far from being physically or logically necessary, self-sufficient or self-explanatory, it is ultimately to be understood from its contingence upon God beyond itself. He pointed to the Genesis account of creation by the majestic *fiat* of God: "Let there be". This means that, although acts of divine creation took place timelessly, the creative commands of God gave rise to orderly arrangements and sequences and enduring structures in the world of time and space. It was the voice of God in creation that called forth the laws of nature. That is to say, all laws of nature, all its intelligible order, are to be regarded as dependent on the Word of God as their ultimate source and ground.

Even physical law points beyond itself to a transcendent ground of intelligibility in the Mind or Word of God the Creator, and it is upon that ground that its constancy as well as its order reposes. According to Basil man himself belongs in body and mind to the realm of contingent being, but as created in the image of God he is the one being made to "look up" to God, and so to be the rational constituent within the created order through whom the secret of its purpose in the wise providence of God may be known. It is through the peculiar place of man on the boundary between heaven and earth, the invisible and the visible, that the rational order in the physical and moral laws of the universe deriving from God may be discerned. This concept of order presupposes an ultimate ground of order transcending what we can comprehend but of which we are dimly aware in our minds under the constraint of which human beings generate order in all rational activity, such as the formulation of laws.

Now let us turn to John Philoponos of Alexandria in the sixth century, the first great Christian physicist whose theological understanding of creation out of nothing led him to question the notion of the eternity of the world put forward by Platonic and Aristotelian thinkers and to apply a powerful conception of contingence to a scientific understanding of the cosmos, evident for example in his *De opificio mundi*, indebted to Basil's *Hexaemeron*, his *De aeternitate mundi contra Proclum*, and his *De aeternitate mundi contra Aristotelem*. By contingence he meant that as freely created by God out of nothing the cosmos has no self-existence and no inherent stability of its own, but is nevertheless endowed by the Creator with an authentic reality and an intelligible order which points beyond itself, and is as such the ground of (empirical) scientific inquiry. By contingent order is meant, then, that the orderly universe is not self-sufficient or ultimately self-explaining but is given a rationality and reliability in its orderliness dependent on and reflecting God's own eternal rationality and reliability.

My concern now is particularly with the way in which, within that general perspective, Philoponos sought to apply the theological distinction between uncreated light and created light to his understanding of the created order.[58] In doing so, he came up with the discovery that light has weight, and that light moves at what he called at a timeless or practically infinite speed! John Philoponos then offered an account of time and space in terms of the movement of light, which was an astonishing anticipation of relativity theory. His importance for our consideration here, however, is with his suggestion on the analogy of the relation between created and uncreated light that the visible things came forth from the invisible. Hence we do not explain the invisible in terms of the visible, but the visible in terms of the invisible. This applies to law, physical and moral law alike, for the rational order which they involve derives from and points back to an ultimate ground of invisible order in God.

---

[58] See the excerpts made by Walter Böhm from the works of Philoponos about light, *Johannes Philoponos, Grammatikos von Alexandrien*, München, 1967, pp. 56f, 103, 185, 195, 307ff, 315f, 419f.

What does this say about World Order? The cosmos with its "world order" is in no sense an emanation from God or necessary for his existence as God. God was under no compulsion to create the universe, and the universe has no reason in itself why it has to be and continue to be what it actually is and becomes. The universe is described as *contingent*, therefore, for it depends entirely on God for its origin, and what it continues to be in its existence and order. The baffling thing about the created universe is that since it came into being it contains no reason in itself why it should be what it is and why it should continue to exist: it is not self-contained, self-sufficient or self-explaining, *although it would not be possible to demonstrate this from within the contingent nature and order of universe itself.* It is ultimately to be understood from beyond itself in its relation to the Creator. Far from being closed in upon itself, the universe is intrinsically open and elusive in its existence and structure, and constantly surprising in its manifestation of new features and patterns.

It was, then, in the light of what became disclosed in this way about the nature and rationality of the creation, that Christian theology laid the basis for a new understanding of the nature and order of the universe. This they found to be neither accidental nor necessary, but as characterized by an inherent intelligibility which could not be construed in terms of either necessity or chance. As already indicated the term they employed here was ἐνδεχόμενος suggested by Athanasius, to express the *contingent* character of created nature and its intelligible order. This was a profound movement of thought which had the epoch-making effect of altering the very foundations of knowledge and science in the ancient world, and of laying the epistemological basis of what we now call empirical science, for it meant that cosmic realities and events may be understood only in accordance with their actual nature, κατὰ φύσιν, through heuristic science, εὑρετικὴ ἐπιστήμη.

The concept of contingence was taken up by Boethius in the West who rendered the Greek verb ἐνδέχεται by the Latin *contingit* and gave us the term "contingent". However, under the guidance of Aristotelian philosophy and logic it was understood in relation to the concept of συμβεβηκός or the "accidental" on the one hand and to the concept of ἀνάνκη or "necessity" on the other hand, and as such was not regarded as subject to true scientific knowledge. Contingent events thus came to be regarded by the Latins as irrational chance events. It was in that Boethian way that contingence was understood and used by St Thomas in developing the relations between Christian theology and Aristotelian science. He operated with the classical model of science, *more geometrico*, according to which the object of scientific investigation must be necessary and universal, together with the Aristotelian way of relating matter, form and causality - everything particular, incidental or accidental being excluded from genuine knowledge. It was by John Duns Scotus that the contingent nature and order of the created order was given its best expression, but it was unfortunately not Scotist but Thomist thought that came to prevail for centuries in western science.

2

Modern science devoted to the investigation of empirical phenomena could not have arisen in the classical form given to it by Galileo and Newton if it had been restricted to a purely *a priori* approach. It arose out of the way of understanding of the universe as created by God and endowed by him with a created or contingent rationality of its own dependent upon his transcendent rationality. This means that while the contingence of the universe cannot be demonstrated from the world itself nevertheless scientific understanding of it is reached only through giving attention to the universe itself, apart from God. And yet - this is a baffling feature about contingence - the independence of the universe from God is itself dependent on God and is sustained by him. That coupling and decoupling of the contingent universe with God lies deep in the foundations of our western science, but the decoupling loses its significance when its relation to the coupling of God and science is neglected or severed, as happened in the Enlightenment. That is the problem, as I see it, of the history of empirical science since the seventeenth century. Empirical science rests upon the concept of the contingent nature and order of the universe which does not contain a sufficient explanation within itself, yet it was pursued through the development of self-explanatory modes and systems of thought in the development of non-contingent necessitarian conceptions of the universe, which threatened the very base upon which it rested and had to go on resting as empirico-theoretic science. However, that is not the whole story, for the all-important empirical ingredient in our science, knowledge of things strictly in accordance with their nature, kept prompting the development of scientific inquiry into the intrinsic intelligibility of things, and demanding new modes of rational formalization appropriate to them. Epistemological and scientific reconstruction of that kind has actually been going on since the middle of the 19th century, with the result that the concept of contingence and contingent rationality has steadily been forcing its way back through the hard crust of necessitarian and determinist thought which overlay it. I would like now to point to several areas in the development of science where contingence has increasingly become evident, and where contingent order is found by science to belong to the essential nature of the universe.

It is to James *Clerk Maxwell* that we must turn first.[59] In his account of the behavior of light and electro-magnetism he developed the concept of the continuous dynamic field as an independent reality in which he broke away from the mechanistic interpretation of nature elaborated in Newton's system of the world. Instead of thinking in terms of particles acting externally on one another, he thought of them as continuously and dynamically interlocked with one another spreading with a velocity equal to the velocity of light. This called for a way of thinking not analytically from parts to a whole but from a "primitive whole" to constituent parts which led to new experimental facts and required a new

---

[59]   Consult my edition of his *A Dynamical Theory of the Electromagnetic Field*, Edinburgh, 1982.

mathematical *mathesis*.[60] This he set out in mathematical equations representing the dynamic structure of the field. According to Einstein the discovery of the mathematical properties of light and the formulation of these differential equations constituted the most important event in the history of physics since Newton's time, not least because they formed the pattern for a new type of law. In this way *Clerk Maxwell probed into a deeper level of intelligibility, disclosing a new reality, a concept for which there was no place in a merely mechanistic description of nature.* Thus he began to uncover something of the contingent nature of the intelligibility that permeates the created universe. *Contingent events cannot be treated like random or chance events, for they have a distinctive intelligibility or order of their own but one nevertheless accessible to appropriate mathematical formulation.* How are they then to be coordinated with the chains of physical causes formulated in classical physics, and with the concept of a final cause? Causal connections, Clerk Maxwell argued, have to be looked at on two different levels, a lower level where subordinate centres of causation operate, and a higher level where we have to do with the operation of a *central cause*, the first being treated as a limiting case of the second. In his investigations the scientist, he said, has to focus "the glass of theory and screw it up sometimes to one pitch of definition and sometimes to another, so as to see down into the different depths", otherwise everything merges dimly together.[61] Thus through a proper adjustment of "the telescope of theory" he is enabled to see beyond the subordinate fact of physical acts and their immediate consequences, to the central focus or cause where he is concerned with the original act behind all subordinate causal connections. However, far from thinking of this final cause as the unmoved Mover in the medieval concept of *Prima Causa* or the absolute inertial framework of the Newtonian system, Clerk Maxwell thought of it after the analogy of a *moral* or *personal* centre of activity, that is to God the Creator. As a convinced Christian he understood this central cause or focus of reference in the light of the dynamic nature of the living God revealed in the incarnation of his Son in Jesus Christ. Thus for Clerk Maxwell the contingent nature of the world brought to light in his dynamical theory of the electromagnetic field called for a new and deeper way of coupling thoughts of God and science. We must not overlook here the fact that the finite speed of the propagation of light and electromagnetic waves carried with it an understanding of the universe as finite in nature and extent and thus as not self-sufficient or self-explanatory but as pointing beyond itself altogether. Thus with Clerk Maxwell the notion of contingence, smothered in classical physics and mechanics, broke out once more into the open in a decisive way demanding scientific recognition.

---

[60] See especially *A Treatise on Electricity and Magnetism*, Dover Edition, London, 1954, vol. 1, p. lxf, and vol. 2, pp. 174-177.

[61] See Lewis Campbell and William Garnett, *The Life of James Clerk Maxwell, with a selection from his correspondence and occasional writings and a sketch of his contribution to science, London,* 1882, pp. 226, 237ff.

We turn next to *Albert Einstein*, and the epistemological revolution brought about by general relativity theory in the integration of empirical and theoretical factors in scientific inquiry. With his comprehensive distinction between absolute and relative, true and apparent, Newton had operated with a radical dualism, in which empirical and theoretical factors were related externally to one another; thus he explained physical features of the world within the rigid framework of Euclidean geometry, a theoretical system of necessary relations independent of time and space. This led to a determinist closed-structured system built up out of static concepts, but it was one which Einstein had been undermined by Clerk Maxwell's concept of the continuous dynamic field. Moreover, with the rise of four-dimensional geometries of space and time, Einstein pointed to the damaging effect of Euclidean geometry as an idealized abstraction from empirical reality. It had been erected into a self-contained conceptual system, pursued as a purely theoretic science antecedent to physics in which we develop our actual knowledge of the world. Rather must geometry be lodged in the heart of physics, where it is pursued as a non-Euclidean geometry in indissoluble unity with physics as the sub-science of its inner rational or epistemological structure and as an essential part of its empirico-theoretical description of reality. While integrated with space-time reality in this way as a "natural science" geometry is not a conceptual system complete in itself, and is consistent as geometry only as it is completed beyond itself in integration with the material content of physics. It is the real geometry of a finite but unbounded universe.

All this implied a rather different view of mathematics which led Einstein to argue that as far as the propositions of mathematics refer to reality they are not certain; and as far as they are certain, they do not refer to reality.[62] Perhaps the most important inference to be drawn here is a negative one: logic closely related to Euclidean geometry is suitable for flat spaces but not for curved ones. This calls for a more realist logic along with a more realist mathematics appropriate to the actual nature of our space-time universe. It was realization of this profound concord between mathematical thinking and the intrinsic intelligibilities of nature that enabled Einstein to resist the pressure to apriorism in his development of relativity theory.

Here let me refer to an issue that appears to be particularly significant for our discussion. It concerns the way in which Einstein, as interpreted by Hermann Weyl, generalized the role given to light by Clerk Maxwell, attributing to it a unique metaphysical as well as physical status in the universe. In the case of all bodies in motion, motion is defined relationally in terms of space and time, while space and time are defined relationally in terms of light. Light itself, however, is not defined in relation to anything else, for its status is unique: here our science comes to a meaningless stop! Or does it? In a very interesting lecture in 1929 "On the Present State of Field-Theory" he argued that in pressing toward the goal of an ultimate logical uniformity we do not just want to know *how* nature is, but want to know *why nature is what is and not otherwise*. No doubt, he granted,

---

[62]   See "Geometry and Experience", *Ideas and Opinions, New York, 1954*, p. 233.

there is a Promethean element lodged in the very concept of logical uniformity for it implies understanding empirical lawfulness as logical necessity even for God! This is an area in scientific reflection, the inner core of nature's secrets, which he claimed to find continually fascinating; it is so to speak, he said, *"the religious basis of the scientific enterprise"*. In raising the question *why?* Einstein was asking a question, set aside during the Enlightenment, about the *ultimate reason* or justification for the laws of nature. He that far from being self-explanatory, the laws of nature are finally open-structured and are contingent upon an ultimate rational ground of order beyond themselves. In theological terms Einstein's *why?* indicates that natural laws as laws of the contingent universe have a limited validity, and are what they ultimately are as *laws* by reference to the commanding and unifying rationality of God the Creator and Sustainer of the universe. Unlike Clerk Maxwell Einstein did not think of this in a personal way, but his frequent references to "God" indicate something of his appreciation of the open contingent character of the universe and its limitless, and indeed `transcendent' nature of its incomprehensible *Verständlichkeit*, or its rational order. That was reinforced by his acceptance of the incompleteness theorem of Kurt Gödel which showed, as Bertrand Russell expressed it, that we must think in terms of a series of rational levels that are open to one another upward but are not reducible downward.

It was with *quantum theory* that the biggest break with the strict causality of classical physics took place, so that the way was opened for a deeper appreciation of contingence through recognition of the elusive non-determinist, and apparently discontinuous, behavior of wave-particles in the sub-atomic structure of nature.

As I see it the main issue was pin-pointed by Einstein in his reaction against the idea that nature acts discontinuously so that in abandoning the strict causality of classical physics resort had to be made to a way of accounting for the behavior of sub-quantum particles only through the calculation of statistical probabilities, which has in fact proved remarkably successful empirically. Empirico-theoretical science, as Einstein understood it, has to do with the apprehension and description of realities themselves at a rather deeper level of intelligibility, and not merely with the probability of their occurrence, far less just with our observations of their occurrence. In his belief that God does not play dice, Einstein was accused of lapsing back into determinism, but that, I believe, was an unfortunate misunderstanding, for as Wolfgang Pauli showed in an important letter to Max Born, Einstein was a "realist", "not a determinist" -and that has since been confirmed in Bell's theorem. In quantum theory Einstein called for a form of continuous, dynamic relatedness inherent in reality, such as had forced itself upon him in relativity theory, but that meant operating with a rather different and deeper conception of rational order for which both classical causality and a chance-necessity, or an indeterminism-determinism dialectic, were irrelevant. Einstein was not rejecting causal connections as such, without which we cannot get on at all, but he wanted a deeper more refined dynamic concept of causality, which he called *Übercausalität*, a principle of super-causality, calling for "new mathematical thinking", really appropriate to the subtle nature of things and their intelligible inter-relations. Hence, as he regarded it, the development of quantum theory required a really deep change in the basic structure of scientific thought. For Einstein it was a *realist* coordination of mathematics in an *appropriate* way with the rational structures of the empirical world that probes into the contingent character and nature of its order, and thereby discloses the deep levels of intelligible relations embedded in empirical realities. This calls for a closer consideration of what Eugene Wigner "the Unreasonable Effectiveness of Mathematics in the Natural Sciences."

Mathematicians are, it is claimed, either formalists or realists. In that distinction the formalists regard mathematics as reducible to a strictly logical system of propositions without ontological reference beyond themselves, and the so-called "realists" are not really realists, but idealists, for the "real" entities to which they hold mathematics to refer are of a Platonic kind. That is to say they do not operate with the Judaeo-Christian view that *creatio ex nihilo* applies not only to matter but to rational, including mathematical, *form*, as well as matter. It was that insight which originally gave rise to the conception of the contingent nature of the universe and its rational order upon which all our empirical science ultimately rests. In mathematics, of course, we elaborate symbolic systems as refined instruments by which we may extend the range of our thought beyond what we are capable of without them. The significance of mathematical symbolisms, however, is to be found not in the mathematical equations themselves but in their bearing upon non-mathematical reality. As far as I can see, mathematics is effective in the physical sciences because *it belongs to the actual contingent world, and reflects and expresses the patterned intelligibilities embodied in it, even though they cannot be captured in abstract mathematical form.* That is why Clerk Maxwell had called for a mathematics of "embodied" kind concerned with "physical relation" and "physical truth". I link this with Einstein's point cited above that if mathematical propositions are certain they are not real, and if they are real they are not certain. In their coordination with the dynamic space-time structure of physical or empirical reality, mathematical propositions share with the universe its open structure - which - far from being false belongs to their truth.

Mathematics rigorously used does not lead to a closed necessitarian or self-explaining system of the world which lends itself to aprioristic thinking, but to an open contingent universe. Whenever mathematics is regarded as intimately correlated with the structures of the empirical universe it operates with open-textured or incomplete symbols, for in rigorous operation it is found to have a reference outside its own system which limits the validity of its formalization. That insight ranges across modern science from Blaise Pascal through Georg Cantor to Kurt Gödel and Alan Turing, but it eluded some of the greatest mathematicians of modern times, Karl Gauss and David Hilbert. With reference to mathematical proof Pascal pointed out that it is impossible to operate only with explicit definitions, for in defining anything in one set of terms we must tacitly assume other terms that remain undefined; to define them we have to presuppose still other terms, and so on in an endless process. Thus even in the strictest mathematical operations we rely upon informal thought-structures, but these informal structures become known only as we rely upon them in developing formal structures. This applies, for example, to the all-important concept of order with which we operate at the back of our minds in all rational and scientific activity but cannot prove, for we have to assume order in all proof and disproof.

Let me refer here to the development of an arithmetic of the infinite, and of set-theory by Georg Cantor, a Jewish Christian mathematician in Halle, born of Danish parents. He regarded a completed set as an infinite magnitude, but he distinguished it as *transfinite* in contrast to the absolute infinity of God. He held that mathematics has to do with a form of rationality which God has imposed upon both the human mind and the universe. It is created harmony between them that gives the universe its rational unity. Hence mathematical deductions from rational structures in the created universe open the way to further discoveries, yet in such a way that finally they point transfinitely beyond themselves. Cantor produced a classical example of contingent rationality when he drew his distinction between transfinite numbers, which exist in the human mind, and the absolute uncreated infinity, which is beyond all human determination and exists only in the mind of God. Since the universe freely created by God might have been other than it is, no scientific deduction from nature must necessarily be so, for it depends upon a transfinite explanation beyond itself.

This brings us to the thought of Kurt Gödel in his famous 1931 essay "On formally undecidable propositions of *Principia Mathematica* and related systems". In *Principia Mathematica* Whitehead and Russell had tried to transcribe pure mathematics into a completely formalized consistent system of logical notions and relations. Gödel showed that this was not the case, by demonstrating that in any formalized system of sufficient richness there are, and must be, certain propositions which are not capable of proof or disproof within the given system, and therefore that it cannot be decided within the system whether the axioms of the system are consistent or mutually contradictory. Thus he demonstrated the inherent limitation of the axiomatic method in which all arithmetical truths are logically derived from a determinate set of axioms. The consistency of such a formal system, if it is consistent, cannot be demonstrated by a proof within it. If it is consistent it is incomplete. Moreover, in line with Cantor, Gödel showed that the true source of the incompleteness attaching to formal systems of mathematics is to be found in the fact that the formation of ever higher types can be continued into the transfinite. Thus undecidable propositions presented in formal systems become decidable through coordination with higher types. A similar result holds for the axiom system of set theory. This demonstrates that in the last analysis we operate in formal systems with basic concepts and axioms which cannot be completely defined, so that we cannot know what the axioms ultimately mean - their truth and meaning lie ultimately beyond themselves. Thus Gödel brought the insights of Pascal and Cantor about the ultimate openness of mathematical propositions and relations to definite proof.

We must coordinate with Gödel's incompletability theorem the brilliant work of Alan M. Turing who through an idealized computing machine tested the provability of certain mathematical theorems, and came up with the discovery of *incomputable* numbers and statements.[63] These statements are incomputable not simply because like mathematical statements in Cantor's transfinite set-theory they require an infinite time to compute, but because, although they may be true, they are inherently non-computable. With Cantor we have to do with contingent intelligibilities which finally outstrip the grasp of our minds for they impinge upon them from beyond the created order, from the absolute infinity of God the Creator. Gödel was influenced by Cantor's concept of transfinite relations in set theory, but his incompletability theorem both vindicated Cantor and reinforced his recognition of the *transcendent ground of order* on which mathematics ultimately relies for its effectiveness in natural science. These developments certainly deal a mortal blow to purely logicist views of mathematics, but from far from undermining mathematics they actually strengthen it and contribute to our understanding of its effectiveness. Let me cite here a statement from John Barrow's 1988 article on "The Mathematical Universe". "If the universe is mathematical in some deep sense, then the mysterious undecidabilities demonstrated by Gödel and Turing are part of the fabric of the universe rather than merely products of our minds. They show that even a mathematical universe is more than axioms, more than computation, more than logic - and more than mathematicians can know."[64]

All this has given considerable impetus to the return of mathematico-scientific thought to an understanding of the nature and rationality of the universe as *open-structured and contingent*, thereby restoring to their integrity the very foundations upon which classical and modern science rest. The consistence and completeness theorems of Gödel and the non-computable functions of Turing, apply, of course, not simply to mathematics and mathematical science, but to the whole mathematical universe, understood as open-ended and incomplete, yet as completed beyond itself transfinitely in absolute Infinity.

By its open-structured contingent nature the orderly universe points to God as the transcendent ground of all order. We have to do here with a *semantic* not a logical reference, however. In the nature of the case there can be no *logical* argument from a contingent universe to its Creator, for as contingent the universe is not self-existent and does not contain a sufficient reason for itself - otherwise it would not be contingent, but would be self-existent and necessary.

3

Let us consider again the coordination of mathematics and physical science, and think of this from the theological perspective not only of the creation but of the incarnation of the creative Word of God within time and space. Through the incarnation time and space are correlated closely with the ultimate rational

---

[63]   See A.M. Turing, *The Mind's I* (ed. D.R. Hofstadter & D.C. Dennett), Basic Books, Middlesix, 1981.

[64]   *Natural Science*, May 1989, p. 311.

ground and the endless possibilities of the Creator. This explains why nature is endowed with the contingent kind of rational order that constantly surprises us in its manifestation of unexpected features and structures which could not be deduced from what is already known, but which always turn out to be consistent with other features and structures already known. What else is this but a manifestation of the contingent intelligibility of the created order? We have to do here with the astonishing flexibility and multivariability of the universe arising out of the correlation of the contingent freedom of the created order with the transcendent freedom of the Creator. That has the effect of reversing the classical approach to physical law, for it means that physical laws are to be formulated under conditions of contingence, where contingence is held to be not just an essential presupposition but a constitutive factor in the mathematical structure of physical law. What we need, therefore, is a new kind of realist mathematical thinking.

Further consideration may now be given to two questions: 1) the bearing of mathematics upon contingent order; 2) and the nature of time in the contingent universe.

1) We have noted that in its coordination with physical reality rigorous mathematics proves to have an open-ended character reflecting the contingent nature of the created world order and its reference beyond itself. A two-way relation is involved here between mathematics and contingence, for it is conformity of mathematics in an *appropriate* way to the contingent nature of physical reality that gives it its heuristic thrust in scientific inquiry. This means that more attention should be given to the distinctive kind or mode of intelligibility that permeates the created order. The need for this becomes apparent when scientists again and again fall back upon the notion of chance, even when they seek to counteract its irrationality through repairing to statistical law. As we have already noted, resort to chance is really a way not to think even when it is coupled with necessity, for it cuts short rational probing into deeper levels of intelligibility. Perhaps at best appeal to chance may be a way of pointing to independent modes of elusive intelligibility beyond the scope of hitherto law, and so indicate that physical laws are what they finally are through a reference beyond themselves to what cannot be defined in terms of these laws. That would bring us back to the notion of incompletability and incomputability disclosed through rigorous mathematical operations. However, it is not enough to bring our thinking to a halt there. We must give more attention to *contingence*, not simply as a factor at the boundary conditions of world order where our abstract mathematical thinking breaks off, but as a primary and profound kind of intelligibility immanent in world order for which we must develop *new forms of thought* appropriate to its subtle elusive nature. A primary feature of the intelligible nature of contingent order is that it is not timeless but temporal, and cannot therefore be properly grasped and explained in conceptual or mathematical forms of thought which do not take that into account. But does time have a distinctive rational order of its own. Is there an order of time - a τάξις χρόνου?

2) This brings me to the problem of trying to understand an essentially *dynamic*, continuously expanding, universe through the deployment of static timeless concepts in mathematics and logic - which seems to me to lie, in part at least, behind some of the bizarre difficulties arising in so-called "chaos theory". This was a problem bequeathed to science through the Newtonian System of the world conceived in terms of the static absolutes of time and space. That was only partially overcome through the relativistic understanding of space-time, where time still remains an external operator, for the dualism between particle and field has not been entirely resolved away, as Einstein hoped. Attempts have now been made, however, to bring what Bergson called "real time" and Prigogine calls "internal time", not the abstract metric time of classical physics, into the central focus and thrust of scientific inquiry.

Real on-going time, which, in metaphorical parlance `flows' or `passes', is intrinsic to all contingent reality and must be interpreted as such, with an open structure like all contingent forms of order. Time thus understood is elusive and cannot be objectified but requires appropriate modes of apprehension and articulation, and as such needs to be brought into scientific inquiry, not as a linear instrument for measuring velocities, but as an internal dynamic functioning of contingent order. In the real on-going time of the expanding universe continuity and novelty bear upon one another under a sort of "invisible hand" or in a kind of spontaneous feed-back way. I think here particularly of the work of Ilya Prigogine and his collaborators in their account of non-equilibrium thermodynamics, which has led them to develop dynamic notions of being as *becoming*, and to speak of "the redemption of time" in the emergence of richer patterns of order arising spontaneously upon the random or disorderly fluctuations that occur far from a state of equilibrium. To express this they have put forward mathematical equations for the passage of thought between dynamic and thermodynamic states of matter, but even here, as far as I am able to judge, while time is brought as an internal operator into physics, real time relations are still not built into the warp and woof of mathematical induction and explanation. That is certainly understandable in respect of traditional mathematics. But what we need is a radically new way of dynamical reasoning in mathematics in which *real time relations* belong to and operate within the basic equations and structures of mathematics.

Similarly what we need is an adaptation of traditional logic formed in connection with classical notions of substance and causality in order to cope with the kind of intelligible relations that obtain in dynamic fields of reality. We now require something like a *logic of verbs* adapted to *becoming* rather than *static being*, logic in which *time* is built as an essential factor into the inner process of reasoning. As far as I am aware, the nearest that has been produced in this respect is the work on *tense logic* initiated by the late A. N. Prior.[65] The problem had already been raised by Kierkegaard in relation to the notion of "becoming" in the

---

[65]   See Mogens Wegner and Peter Øhrstrøm, "A New Tempo-Modal Logic for Emerging Truth", J. Faye et al. (Eds) *Perspective on Time*, 1997, pp. 417-441.

Johannine statement "the Word *became* flesh". This requires a kinetic mode of thought appropriate to the movement (*kinesis*) of the Word in *becoming* flesh in time and space, and that calls for *movement* to be to be given a central place in the categories governing all thinking in time and space. The effect of this would be to give the categorical structure of the understanding a dynamic rather than a static character, and to obviate the transposition of temporal into logical relations.

In working this out Kierkegaard found he had to abandon a way of thinking from a point of absolute rest, which was a way of "thinking movement or becoming by abrogating it", and develop a new dynamic yet realist way of thinking in which he could be true to objective movement, whether in God's interaction with us in time and space or in any authentic historical event, without the *metabasis eis allo genos* of converting becoming into necessity.

That was an astonishing anticipation of the way that modern physics was to take, but unfortunately Kierkegaard was seriously misunderstood in the rise of existentialist philosophy according to which there was no inherence of *logos* in *phusis* or any notion of the intrinsic intelligibility of empirical events. There had to take place a rejection of the Kantian *synthetic a priori* as a way of coordinating theoretical and empirical factors in knowledge while maintaining the disjunction between them, and at the same time the realization that contingent events have an inherent objective intelligibility in the light of which they are to be understood and explained. That is precisely what took place with general relativity theory which demolished Newton's dualism between two kinds of time, absolute mathematical time and relative apparent time. Epistemologically the effect of general relativity was to heal the breach between geometry and experience, and to show that theoretical and empirical factors inhere in one another in nature itself and in every level of our scientific knowledge of it, and thus to lay the basis for a unitary understanding of the world as finite and unbounded. This implies, not only that empirical events are essentially contingent, but that they are endowed with a contingent intelligibility of their own, and that therefore historical events are properly to be interpreted not in terms of alien patterns of thought clamped down upon them *ab extra*, but in terms of the distinctive rational order they possess in their own right. The particular importance of this Einsteinian revolution for our understanding of history was the deliverance of real motion and real time from their mathematical analysis into still small points strung together in linear connection in accordance with rigid logico-mathematical law. Everything changes when the empirical and the mathematical are intrinsically coordinated with the continuous objective structure of the on-going universe, for then we may seek to understand motion and time only through abandoning a point of absolute rest, and removing the possibility of reducing what we understand to closed conceptual explanations of abstract mathematical formalizations.

When the equations of general relativity predicting their own ultimate limits were matched by empirical evidence of the microwave background radiation, it became evident that the universe had been expanding for some fifteen billion years, more or less, from an originally incredible dense state. This beginning of the world, Einstein held, "really constitutes a beginning". This led Henry

Margenau of Yale to show that the equations of general relativity theory have the effect of negating objections to the biblical concept of *creatio ex nihilo,* with which Einstein himself agreed. It became clear that the universe was in fact an immense, and of course unique, historical event with a real beginning. This has helped to force *real ongoing time* back into the essential subject-matter of scientific inquiry and knowledge. It is now evident that all scientific inquiry within the on-going expansion of the universe has to do with time-dependent dynamic order. This reinforces the conviction that world order is fundamentally contingent not only in its nature but in its inherent rationality and temporality. All scientific truths and all physical laws are as contingent as the universe itself. In that case rather baffling problems have to be faced: how to meet the compelling claims of contingent structures in nature and its history through appropriate formulations of scientific truth, and in particular how to write time into the fundamental equations of physical law. As we have already noted this calls for a new kind of embodied mathematics. Mathematical formulations of rational structures embedded in the time-space continuum of the universe must take the form of incomplete symbols, which to be consistent have to have a reference outside their own system in limitation of their formal validity but not of their truth. That is to say, time is what it is by relation beyond itself to what is not temporal but eternal, so that the *order of time* (τάξις χρόνου) must be of a teleological kind, with a beginning and an end.

What then is *time*? We all know what time is, for we all experience time as a form of life and existence, but we do not know what we are saying when we say "time"![66] As time belongs to the contingent nature and order of the created universe, we must try to grasp and interpret it in accordance with what it is in itself, and yet since it was created by God out of nothing along with the universe, we must allow our relation with God to play a role in our understanding of time. As we have seen, that applies to the very notion of contingence which by its very nature is neither self-sufficient nor self-explanatory - its origination, ground and sufficient reason lie outside the universe, in God. This does not mean that we have to reject empirico-scientific approach to an understanding time, for as with the universe created out of nothing, we must look away from God in order to know it in accordance with its contingent otherness. So far, however, scientific inquiry has not been able to carry us much beyond reference to time as a standard for the measurement of velocity, which gives rise to an abstract metric concept of time. It is the contingent nature of time, created with the world out of nothing, which makes it so elusive for us to grasp. This is particularly difficult for science. While time is intrinsically real, as real as anything else in the created universe, and must be understood properly in accordance with its own intelligible reality, by its very nature time cannot be objectified and described by us, any more than we can capture the present moment, a progressive "now-point" in the stream of

---

[66]   Cf. St. Augustine, *Confessions* XI, 14: "What then *is* time? If no one asks me, I know; if I want to explain it to a questioner, I do not know." Tr. By F.J.Sheed, London, 1949.

our experience, which is no sooner present than it is gone. Yet all the time, time keeps on flowing, coming, or going.

We recall that it was when working with the distinction between the uncreated light of God and the created light of the world that John Philoponos was able to overthrow Platonic and Aristotelian notions of the eternity of the world, and to make such astonishing progress in the physics of light. It also led him to reject Aristotle's idea of measuring motion by time and time by motion, although he held that time and motions are devised for one another like relative concepts. John Philoponos brought to full development early Christian doctrine of the creation of the world out of nothing, which has a beginning and an end, and of the intelligible nature and unitary order of all things visible and invisible under God, including the contingent nature and reality of time, unceasingly upheld through and in the Word of God incarnate in Christ. May it not be helpful, then, to operate with a parallel distinction between created time and uncreated "time", that is, between the created time of the universe defined by its contingent nature, and the uncreated "time" (so to speak) of the eternal life of God defined by his divine nature, in the hope that this may enable us to grasp something of *the reality, nature, and order of contingent time?*

As a Christian theologian I believe that we must reflect more realistically about the implications of the Incarnation, of God the Creator personally incarnate in time and space, and his redemptive purpose in the history of the world. God's coming among us and as one of us was an utterly astonishing event, something quite new, not only for the created world order, but even for the ever living God![67] The fact that though God was always Father he was not always Creator, and the fact that though he was not always incarnate he became incarnate in Jesus Christ, means that there is a "before" and "after" in the eternal life of God, and thus a kind of divine "time", identical with the ever living and ever acting God. What are the implications of this, especially of the Incarnation of God the Creator become creature in time and space, of the eternal become temporal, for our understanding of time?

The incarnation of God himself, the Creator of heaven and earth, in Jesus Christ, in the time and space of created world order, means that a deeper ontological bond has been forged between uncreated time and created time, which undergirds its contingency and establishes its ongoing nature, reality, and order in a new way. Here we think of the eternal time of God incarnate as penetrating and embracing the contingent time of our creaturely world thereby giving it features which it does not have merely in virtue of its creaturely nature. What are these features?

In the first place, the ongoing time of our passing world has been given a fortified reality - it is not something merely contingent that is subjected to random chance and futility. While time has been created along with the world as

---

[67]   For the following refer to the thinking of Athanasius about this which I explain in *The Trinitarian Faith, The Evangelical Theology of the Ancient Catholic Church*, Edinburgh, 1995 reprint, pp. 84ff.

having a contingent reality, it is not left to its contingence away from God, but is undergirded and reinforced in its contingent dependence upon the Creator, so that in all its fleeting character it is held together and made to consist in the upholding presence and affirming activity of the Logos or Word of God incarnate in time and space.

In the second place, the ongoing time of our world has been given a real end or goal, a teleological thrust in its direction and order. That was a primary effect of the once and for all nature of the Incarnation, something absolutely decisive for all time. Such an absolute within the empirical relativities of temporal existence and history, with an unrepeatable before and after, changes ongoing time quite fundamentally, decisively, and irreversibly. This is marked for Christians by the dating of historical events before and after Christ, which left such a profound impact upon understanding of historical thinking, thus liberating Greek thought of time from the tyranny of the ever-recurring processes in nature, such as the endless cycle of cosmological events or the continual succession of day and night and the seasons of the year. The fact that in the Incarnation something happened which is decisive for all time and all people, had a revolutionary effect on the concept of history, for history was thereby given an end or a goal. As such history becomes real history emancipated from chance and illusion.

In the third place, we must take into account what St Paul spoke of as *the redeeming of time*. In Jesus Christ God became man in our alienated disorderly world without ceasing to be God, and the eternal became time within the temporal structures of our decaying creaturely existence without ceasing to be eternal, thereby anchoring the world in the redemptive love of God. Our human life is characterized by decay and mortality, for from our birth we are involved in an ineluctable process of decay and sooner or later tumble down into the grave. In some inexplicable way there is evil at work in the universe, giving disorder a crooked twist so that it is not just an entropic feature of nature on the way toward order, but is fraught with destructive tendencies. In this event the redemption of the universe from disorder requires more than a rearrangement of form like the resolving of dissonance in music, namely, the radical defeat and undoing of evil. In Christian theology that is precisely the bearing of the Cross upon the way things actually are in our universe of time and space. It represents the refusal of God to remain aloof from the disintegration of order in what he has made. It is his decisive personal intervention in the world through the Incarnation of his Word and Love in Jesus Christ. In his life and passion he who is the ultimate source and power of all created order has penetrated into the untouchable core of our contingent existence in such a way as to deal with the twisted force of evil entrenched in it, and bring about a redemptive reordering of temporal existence.

Thus in Christian theology we think of the advent of Christ into our temporal and mortal existence within the structures of time and space as having an essentially redemptive purpose with ontological as well as moral implications. This is held to apply not only to the human race but to the whole created world order, in the vanquishing of its latent disorder, in overcoming its estrangement, and in the reconciling of all things visible and invisible to one another in cosmic harmony with the Creator. In the Incarnation of God the embracing of created time by the uncreated time of his eternal life has been established in such a final way that created time can no more vanish back into nothing than God himself can cease to be. But the finalizing of that ontological relation between created time and uncreated time has an intrinsic teleological thrust toward overcoming the irrationality of evil and disorder that have inexplicably invaded the creation. Hence far from negating created time uncreated time fulfils it and enriches its reality. Christian theology thus thinks of the Incarnation of the Creator Logos of God as penetrating back through created time to the very beginning unraveling the twisted skein of evil, recapitulating all things in himself, as St Paul expressed it, in order to liberate us from the tyranny of the guilt-conditioned irreversibility in which our existence has become trapped, and so to heal our existence of disorder and direct it forward to the renewal and consummation of all things in the Creator. This has the effect of giving time a future slant of a teleological as well as an eschatological kind, which is reflected in the way the New Testament speaks of Christ as the First and the Last, whose Advent or *Parousia* (παρουσία) is a coming that is a presence and a presence that is a coming. This implies that in the redemptive purpose of God created time is set on a new basis in which it is given a built-in end yet to be fulfilled. New things happen - new time flows from the end to come which gives a perspective to time and new meaning to the past and to the present. That is *the redemption of time*, for instead of running down, time is directed onward and forward toward an ever higher and richer pattern of order in the promise of a future that will increasingly take us by surprise.

It may be helpful to consider this redemptive effect of the Incarnation upon time in connection with recent development in thermodynamical theory through Katsir, Landsberg, Prigogine and others.

According to the second law of thermodynamics, which applies only to *closed systems*, all physical and chemical processes tend toward an increase of disorder or entropy (ἐντροπή). In its classical form this `law' is of relevance only to macroscopic processes, and does not apply either to microsystems or to the universe as a whole, which seriously limits its usefulness in our understanding of the expansion of the universe, or to the development of living organisms. However, there are now startling developments in the thermodynamics of *open systems* such as living organisms in which, while the classical formulation of the second law for closed isolated systems is not challenged, a restatement of that law on a different level has had to be made to cope with the way in which order is found to emerge in the expanding universe. According to classical thermodynamics increase in order is always at the expense of increase of disorder, which implies that fundamental change takes place irreversibly only in that one direction, even though there are pockets in nature which deviate from this rule. How is it, then, that the whole expansion of the universe shows a steady upward gradient in the emergence of ever richer patterns of order from the `primeval soup' of its earliest minutes to the wonderful complex order of the human brain and indeed, scientific knowledge of the universe? Prigogine and others, who have been mainly responsible for the development of non-equilibrium thermodynamics, have shown that order is found to arise spontaneously upon the random or disorderly fluctuations that occur far from a state of equilibrium, that is, in the behavior of open systems in which an exchange of matter and energy takes place between them and their environment. In a closed determinist world governed by logico-mathematical connections and the statistically formalized laws of thermodynamics, the arrow of time moves with ineluctable increase in entropy or disorder. In the open-structured world of relativistic quantum theory and non-equilibrium thermodynamics, on the other hand, the arrow of time moves in the opposite direction with a spontaneous increase in order and the emergence of new structure. In the former, time is an external parameter governing nature in a geometrically absolute way without being affected by what happens in the empirical world, and as such it closes the door to the future - thus, the future is determined by the present and the past. In the latter, however, time inheres in the empirical world as an essential dynamic property of nature and operates as an internal parameter in its on-going processes, and as such it opens the door to the future - thus the future is indeterminate. In the former the irreversibility of time means that time is *unredeemable*, but in the latter the irreversibility of time means that, as Prigogine expresses it, time is *redeemable*. Thus strangely the law of entropy operates in a closed deterministic way near the state of equilibrium in terms of the disintegration of structure, but in open systems, such as living organisms, it allows for a creative functioning far from the state of equilibrium in terms of the transformation of structure through fluctuation. The paradox is that order should emerge spontaneously, and inexplicably, out of disorder, that is, not in spite of entropy but because of entropy. This happens, for example, with living organisms which are open systems in which matter and energy are exchanged with the environment.

In our theological account of the effect of the incarnation of the Creator Word within the finite time and space of our world, and its decaying disorderly nature, we spoke of it in terms of the way in which the uncreated time of God's eternal life embraces created time, and of its redemptive effect upon created time in bringing order out of disorder. It may help us now in our theologico-scientific approach to creation, contingent order and time, to think of it after the analogy of the way the environment bears creatively upon open systems in such a way as to bring about the spontaneous emergence of new structures of order, thereby redeeming time from being subjected to a deterministic world of ineluctable decay. In Christian theology we hold that in Jesus Christ the order of redemption has intersected the order of our world, judging, forgiving and healing it of malevolent disorder, and making it share in the wholly benign order of the divine life and love. Since in Jesus Christ there became embodied within time the very Word of God by whom all things are made and in whom they cohere, the redemption of time is to be regarded as applying not just to the human race but to the whole created universe of things visible and invisible. If we think of world order as an open system in this kind of way within the redemptive embrace of the uncreated time of the divine life, we cannot but have a different understanding of world order and time. Scientific accounts of creation, world order and time, will inevitably disappoint us if we think of them within the theoretical framework of a closed system that is, of a system closed off from God but it will be quite otherwise if we learn to think of it within the creative and redemptive embrace of the life and love of God. It is to him that the open structures of our contingent world, mathematical and physical, point transfinitely beyond themselves.

4

Moral order has an essential role in world order, if only because it is a form of the rational order with which our minds are attuned in an ultimate belief that, whatever may appear to the contrary in so-called random or chance events, the universe to which we belong is intrinsically orderly, and reflects as such an ultimate ground of order as its all-important sufficient reason. That ultimate ground of order is and must be hidden, for in the nature of the case it cannot be conceptualized - far less explained - in terms of the orderly arrangements within the universe itself that are indebted to it. In a strange way it is known in not being known, or known only in a tacit or subsidiary way as the comprehensive presupposition for the understanding of all order. Without it everything would be meaningless and pointless. This belief in order, together with a refusal to accept the possibility of an ultimate fortuitousness behind the universe, lies deeply embedded in our moral as well as our religious consciousness.

Two points about this moral order may be made. In the first place, it has arisen together with science, art, and religion, as part of the steady expansion of the universe towards richer and higher patterns of order which we seek to understand in rational and scientific inquiry. Hence moral order cannot be set aside in rational and scientific inquiry, for it belongs to the universe, and as such calls for a reconsideration of the nature of nature. The embedding of the human being in nature means that the moral order is not extraneous but essential to the nature of nature and its rational order. In other words, it tells us that moral obligation is ontologically integrated with the commanding intelligibility inherent in the being and becoming of world order.

In the second place, the realization that moral order has a place within the expanding order of the universe is reinforced by the rethinking of classical thermodynamics in application to open systems, in which, as we have noted, order is found emerging spontaneously far from states of equilibrium where instead of random fluctuations or chaos we find more organized or higher levels of order. The kind of order that arises in this way may be regarded as "entropy-consuming": that is an orderly movement against a tendency toward an increase in entropy or disorder. But that is after all, what *science* itself is, an entropy-consuming activity, geared into the entropy-consuming activity of nature, and dedicated to the understanding and maintaining of order in the face of the "natural" inclination of nature to degenerate into states of disorder. Hence it may be said that the inner compulsion which prompts and drives our science is an extension of the rational compulsion under which we human beings live our daily lives. This inner compulsion is what R.B. Lindsay has aptly called "*the thermodynamic imperative*" reflected in the way we feel bound to live and act in producing as much order in our environment as possible, that is, to maximize the consumption of entropy. That is very evident in the relation between pure science and the developing of technology in order to transmute available energy into higher and more complex patterns, through which the inherent forces of nature are encouraged to function in accordance with their own latent possibilities for increase in order. I believe that we must discern behind this imperative to increase the degree of order whether in nature or human life, something much more compelling, a requirement or obligation emanating from the ultimate ground of order and echoed by the claims of created reality upon us. This is the imperative of which we are acutely aware as we tune our minds as faithfully as possible to the intrinsic structures of the universe, for it generates within us what we call the *scientific conscience*. It is an imperative which the scientist as scientist cannot in rational conscience disregard or disobey, but to which he is wholly committed. It is this imperious order, the ontic truth of things to which we are rationally committed and over which we have no control, which stands guard over all our scientific inquiries and theories from discovery to verification. How are we to think of the relation between this *thermodynamic imperative* with which we have to do in natural science and the *categorical imperative* with which we have to do in moral science or ethics, under the commanding authority of the ultimate ground of order? They cannot but belong together and affect one another in world order.

The nub of the problem facing us here is that inherited from the Enlightenment, the deep rift torn in human knowledge between the *how* and the *why*, between the *is* and the *ought*. It is to that rift that the unhappy splits in our modern culture go back, and not least the damaging separation between the physical and the human sciences, or the natural and the moral sciences, and between natural science and theological science. Can we ever reach a unified field theory, even one of an open-structured kind, unless we heal that rift? In order to do that we need to operate within a dimensional perspective which transcends that separation, that is, theologically speaking, from within the relation of *God* to the universe and world order. As Max Planck once claimed, the unified view of the world demanded by science requires in some way coordination between the power of God and the power that gives force to the laws of nature, which would have the effect of giving those laws a definitely teleological character.

As we have seen important developments in fundamental inquiry are already taking place in which rigorous questioning refuses to be halted at artificial barriers laid down in the past by a myopic view of scientific knowledge, and reaches out across the *how* to the *why* and beyond the *is* to the *ought*.

Let us recall again the point made by Einstein that science cannot remain satisfied merely with describing the laws of nature, but must press beyond knowing *how* nature is what it is, to knowing *why* nature is what it is and not something else. That means that rigorous science must be concerned with the inner justification of nature's laws in order to disclose the reasons for them, and so is bound to be concerned with how things *ought* to be as well as with how they actually are. There Einstein was in fact questioning the artificial dichotomy between the *how* and the *why*, and indeed between the *is* and the *ought*, built into western science by the Enlightenment. This implies that the laws of nature are to be understood not just in the way they relate logically to one another but in the light of their relation to an ultimate ground of rational order. As I see it this means that scientific inquiry, whether a scientist is aware of it or not, must conform to the contingent nature of the universe and respect the openness of its immanent rationality to the transcendent Rationality of God the Creator.

Einstein's demand that science must be concerned with the inner reason or ultimate justification of natural law also has powerful implications for the moral and social sciences. This was already evident from the massive recovery of *ontology* in the foundations of knowledge brought about through the integration of theoretical and empirical factors in general relativity theory. Recognition of the coinherence of truth and being in nature and in our knowledge of it, to which this gives rise, radically changes the attitude to *reality* and deepens the sense of obligation generated in the scientific mind under its compelling claims. The effect of this is to call in question the positivist notion of *Wertfreiheit* or value-free science that has become entrenched in the social sciences, together with the separation of the *ought* from the *is* in moral and legal science, and to call for the recovery of ontology in their fields also. This integration of the *ought* with the *is*, must not be confused with "Hume's principle" or the "naturalistic fallacy", i.e. the identification of what may be regarded as natural, factual, or conventional with what is positively obligatory. Instead, it opens the way for an ethic grounded upon an imperative latent in reality in which we not only think and speak of things in accordance with their nature, that is, truly, but act toward them in accordance with their nature, that is, truly. At the same time the way becomes open for realist moral and social science in which questions of truth and falsity are no longer artificially bracketed off from serious investigation. It would thus seem incumbent upon all science for the moral imperative to function as an *internal operator*, and not just in an external utilitarian way.

Once the artificial separation between the "is" and the "ought" is set aside, a profound element of *moral obligation* demands to be built into the essential process of scientific inquiry, so that the "ought" becomes essential to the rational structure of scientific inquiry as a significant factor of control. It will be granted that the scientist finds himself operating under a compelling claim of nature, to which he ought in scientific conscience to yield, but how far is this compelling claim grounded in nature to be understood as a *moral* imperative?

How then are we to think of the relation between natural law and moral law?

We need not be concerned at this particular moment with the divine ground of law, but with its open character. This has become very clear today in realist science in which scientific concepts and theories point beyond themselves to the nature of the objective realities into which we inquire and by which they are governed and in the light of which they continue to be revisable. By their nature realist laws are incomplete and open-structured, for they have their truth in the realities which they indicate beyond themselves, but which they are unable to capture completely within the net of their theoretical concepts and formalizations. The realist objectivity of natural law and its openness belong essentially together. All scientific theories and formulations of natural law, while objective and true, are open-structured and provisional, for the universe, together with its natural laws, cannot be understood completely out of itself, but require an explanatory reference beyond itself. Thus even the most rigorous mathematical equations are intrinsically incomplete and call for completion beyond themselves.

I believe that this applies not only to physical laws, but to moral laws, however axiomatically and logically formalized, for they also derive from and point back to an ultimate rational ground beyond themselves. If moral laws are logically certain they are not necessarily true, but if they are true they are open-structured and may not be subjected without falsification to complete and logically certain formalization. I believe that this is a matter that legal science needs to take into account today, for legal science has too long been infected with positivism, and needs to recover a realist open-structured conception of moral and juridical law.

We must now consider how natural law and moral law are related to one another. This has become very important today for medical science, particularly in the field of genetics where difficult problems arise and crucial decisions have to be made. The basic question that arises here, for example in embryology, is whether research or experimentation with embryos is in the interest of the embryo or in the interest of the scientist in his desire to advance knowledge and his own reputation. This is a clear instance where scientific and moral integrity are inviolably one - any refusal by a scientist to meet the obligation imposed upon him by the nature of what he is investigating is a rejection of the compelling claims of reality upon him. In both science and ethics we are obliged to know things and behave towards them strictly in accordance with their natures, and may not confuse ends with means. The scientific conscience will not allow the scientist to do otherwise. To say the least he is aware of an obligation to be faithful to the actual facts, and may not `cook the results' of his experiments. However, this has also to do with the relation of scientific inquiry to the inner compulsion of the universe in its expansion toward maximum order, the imperative immanent in the natural order to which we with all nature belong. In his commitment to order the scientist is committed to its entelechy toward the maximization of order. That is to say, in his obligation to behave in accordance with the nature of things, the scientist comes under the compelling claim of nature to further its immanent intrinsic thrust toward fuller and richer patterns of order, which he seeks to fulfill through appropriate inquiry and in technological development harnessed appropriately together. But how far may the scientist impose upon nature a pattern of order of his own devising alien to it, if only to satisfy his curiosity? This is the area where pure science and applied science often conflict in confusing ends with means, where strict behavior in accordance with the nature of nature may clash with technological manipulation governed by some professionally or socially desired end. Surely any refusal by a scientist to meet the obligations imposed upon him by the nature of what he is investigating is a rejection of the compelling moral claims of reality upon him.

How then are we to think of the relation between natural law and moral law? Let me recall here the basic principle on which the Royal Society in London was founded, succinctly formulated in its motto, *Nullius in Verba*, in which expression is given to the nature of science pursued strictly on its own ground and under the compelling claims of the realities being investigated, and not on the ground or `say so' of any external authority. Scientific inquiry and discovery are pursued in rigorous attention to the intrinsic intelligibility of nature throughout the universe without imposing extrinsic patterns of thought on our understanding of it. This implies that natural law may not and cannot rightly be related to moral law in any external way, but only on a rational ground and under a compelling authority common to both scientific and moral inquiry, the intrinsic intelligibility of the created universe which points to an ultimate ground of rationality and constancy beyond itself. We have to think and act here under the imperative of an ultimate ground that is both rational and moral. It is only on that common ground that natural and moral law may be related rationally and properly to one another in such a way that each may be true to itself without conflict with the other. That is surely what should happen in the field of medical ethics, where difficult decisions have to be taken but where it is often very difficult today to determine what is morally right, yet merciful and beneficial. This is of crucial importance in genetic engineering which can be of such enormous benefit in treating and even obviating disease. Unfortunately this is not how current science always operates when, for example, appeal is made to some form of utilitarian ethics to justify some `helpful' act of genetic manipulation, which may be backed up by some local statute law, but not by realist common law. Utilitarian ethics is of course the kind of ethics to which all fascist and communist governments appeal in their self-justification. In so doing natural science sins gravely against its own nature and the rigorous rule, *Nullius in Verba*.

The more strictly scientific inquiry concerns itself with the intrinsic intelligibility of the created order, the more it finds it has to operate with open structures or incomplete formalizations which through the nature of their inherent rationality point beyond themselves to an ultimate ground of order. Far from that open or incomplete character being an indication of deficiency or falsity it is found to be essential to their truth. The more profoundly realist scientific theories or formulations of natural law are, the more they indicate much more than they can express, and have their truth beyond themselves, in the light of which they continue to be revisable. I believe it is in much the same way that rigorous moral and legal science operates, under the compulsion of a transcendent ground of rational order to which they point and in the light of which their formulations continue to be revisable.

What are we to make of the fact that both physical law and moral law are what they are in their contingent relation to the ultimate ground of order and function under its commanding imperative? Here let us recall again the fact that all rational and scientific thought presupposes that the universe is inherently orderly, otherwise it would not be understandable or open anywhere to rational investigation and description. This fundamental belief in order is not something that we can prove, for it has to be assumed in all proof and disproof, and arises irresistibly as a decisive operator in our consciousness under the impact of reality from beyond ourselves. As such it is, so to say, built into the inner walls of our minds, and exercises a regulative function in all scientific inquiry, explanation and verification. Within scientific operations we cannot but submit our minds to the compelling claims of reality and its intrinsic rational order, so that we have to reckon not only with an ontological basis for knowledge but with a normative basis with which our scientific intuition resonates. Thus we think rationally and scientifically only as we think under the compelling claims of reality and its intrinsic intelligibility. We find ourselves up against an immanent imperative in nature in response to which we frame our understanding of its objective, dynamic arrangements in terms of physical law, and we are deeply aware of an obligation thrust upon us from the ultimate ground of order which gives rise to the *scientific conscience*.

In holding that both physical and moral law are what they are in their contingent relation to the ultimate ground of order and function under its commanding imperative, we cannot but affirm that there are not, and cannot be, two ultimate grounds of order - we do not live and cannot think rationally within a schizoid universe! No more than we can think of there being two Gods can we think of two ultimate grounds of order, one rational and the other moral, and therefore of two different imperatives laid upon us. However, if physical and moral laws, for all their difference, have a unitary ontological ground beyond themselves, to which they are open and in the light of which they are to be justified, they must also be locked together in the compelling claims they make upon us. This is apparent in the fact that in all inquiry in natural and moral science we are obliged to respect, know and act toward, realities of whatever kind strictly in accordance with their natures in a true and faithful way and not otherwise. All true and right respond to the imperious constraint of a single transcendent reality which we cannot rationally or morally resist. This is surely an essential part of what we mean by *conscience*, whether scientific or moral, the functioning of a moral imperative as an internal operator in the determination of natural and moral law which is both ontologically grounded in the nature of ultimate reality. In other words, the unconditional obligation of which we are aware in our conscience is an ontic as well as a moral obligation. If natural science and ethics overlap in their epistemological and ontological structure at this crucial point, it seems clear that the sharp cleavage between science and ethics commonly accepted since the Enlightenment must be rejected in order to do justice to the double fact that there is an inescapable moral ingredient in scientific activity and an inescapable rational ingredient in ethical behavior. The recognition of their common relation to a unitary intelligible ground in ultimate reality will help to reinforce the moral imperative latent in physical law, and the rational imperative latent in moral law.

I believe that a rethinking and restructuring of fundamental scientific inquiry and method in setting aside the rationalistic dichotomy between the *is* and the *ought*, and an inclusion of the moral imperative as an essential factor of control in an appropriate way within the formulation of natural law is being forced on us at every hand. This is nowhere more evident than in the field of ecological research concerned with the conservation of the planet on which we live. But above all it is becoming more evident day by day in medical science where bioethical issues of the greatest importance for the survival of the human race have been raised. The ground for this change has already been prepared in the recovery of ontology and the role of belief in the foundations of knowledge, but that requires to be nourished through the heuristic vision of an ultimate unitary basis in the rational and moral order of the created universe, to which Christian theology is committed.

Chapter 4

Contingent and Divine Causality[68]

1

My choice of title for this address, *Causa et Prima Causa, Contingent and Divine Causality*, has been influenced by the fact that in recent discussions on both sides of the Atlantic I have found a deep cleft in many people's thought of God and Science, between an older way of thinking that has persisted since Aristotle was introduced into Western thought in the thirteenth century, together with a Euclidean understanding of science *more geometrico*, and a more open-structured yet mathematical understanding of science that was initiated by James Clerk Maxwell. This is evident in the kind of thinking in closed causal and mechanistic connections that still seems to pervade western society, not least as reflected in the media, and the common dualist way of regarding a relation between belief and science which it involves. But this is also found in the failure even of many scientists as well as theologians to appreciate the profound epistemological revolution brought about by dynamic field theory and general relativity theory. The deep divergence latent in modern thought is indicated by *"causa and prima causa"* on the one hand, and by "contingent and divine Causality" on the other hand, although there is here a divergence in the very notion of "cause" that must be taken into account in view of the *contingent* nature of the rational order pervading the space-time universe with which empirico-theoretical science now operates.

The concept of the creation of the universe out of nothing originally derived from the Hebraic tradition, but it was radicalized by the understanding of God's self-revelation in the incarnation and resurrection of his Son in Jesus Christ. He was the Word of God by whom all things were made and without whom no created thing has come into being, and through whom they are endowed with their creaturely order. The notion of *contingence* arose out of the way in which early Greek patristic theology, sought to express the distinctive nature of the universe as freely created in matter and form by God out of nothing, and endowed by him with a reality of its own, utterly different from God yet

[68] Lecture for Conference on "God and Science", King's College, London, April 27, 1996.

dependent on him. It was the startling resurrection of Jesus Christ, the incarnate Son of God, from the dead, that opened the minds of Christian thinkers like Athenagoras of Athens in the second century to the creative power of God over life and death, over being and non being alike.[69] Thus in Christ there became revealed the mighty act of God within the physical and rational structures of his creation; and Christians realized that in him as God and man, the one Mediator between God and man, the exalted Lord over all realities visible and invisible, the Creator has for ever bound the universe to himself as the source of its continued existence and of its created constitution in space and time. The universe proceeded from God not from any internal necessity of his transcendent being or will, but freely out of sheer grace which is not constrained to operate by anything beyond himself. The universe is in no sense an emanation from God or necessary for his existence as God. God was under no compulsion to create the universe, and the universe has no reason in itself why it has to be and continue to be what it actually is and becomes. The universe is described as *contingent*, therefore, for it depends entirely on God for its origin, and what it continues to be in its existence and order. The baffling thing about the created universe is that since it came into being it contains no reason in itself why it should be what it is and why it should continue to exist: it is not self-contained, self-sufficient or self-explaining. It is ultimately to be understood from beyond itself in its relation to the Creator. Far from being closed in upon itself, it is intrinsically open and elusive in its existence and structure, and constantly surprising in its manifestation of new features and patterns.

The incarnation and resurrection were utterly new astonishing events which could be understood only out of themselves. It was in the light of what became disclosed through them about the nature and rationality of the creation, that Christian theology laid the basis for a new understanding of the nature and order of the universe. This they found to be neither accidental nor necessary, but as characterized by an inherent intelligibility which could not be construed in terms of either necessity or chance. The term they employed here was ἐπιδεχόμενος suggested by Athanasius, to express the *contingent* character of created nature and order. This was a profound movement of thought which had the epoch-making effect of altering the very foundations of knowledge and science in the ancient world, and of laying the epistemological basis of what we now call as empirical science. This way of thinking was primarily evident in the way in which Christian theologians tried to grapple with knowledge of the utterly astonishing event of the Incarnation, God himself incarnate in space and time, and so more generally with how to know and understand what is utterly *new, out of itself*, in accordance with its own nature or reality, and not in terms of preconceived ideas.[70] What is really new can be known only out of itself. Thus they advocated a way of inquiry, which they called εὑρετικὴ ἐπιστήμη, or

---

[69] Athenagoras, *Peri Anastaseos*, 3-5; and my discussion, *Divine Meaning. Studies in Patristic Hermeneutics*, Edinburgh, 1995, pp. 51f.

[70] See the *Stromateis* of Clement of Alexandria, and *Divine Meaning*, Ch.6, pp. 130ff.

heuristic knowledge pursued strictly in accordance with the nature (κατὰ φύσιν) or reality (κατ' ἀλήθειαν) of what is being investigated. This called for a new kind of question that yielded positive knowledge, which they called δογματικὴ ἐπιστήμη, or dogmatic science. This was not unlike the kind of inquiry being pursued by the physical scientists (φυσικοί) attacked by Sextus Empiricus, but with Christians it was governed by belief in the positive intelligibility inherent in the created order. This new way of inquiry and knowing was not restricted to Christian theology, and came to be applied at other levels to understanding and interpretation of the created or contingent universe. Here one thinks above all of the works of John Philoponos of Alexandria in the sixth century, such as his *De opificio mundi, De aeternitate mundi contra Proclum,* and *Contra Aristotelem.*

Unfortunately John Philoponos was accused, quite mistakenly, of being a monophysite heretic, with the result that with his rejection his contribution to the development of empirical science was rejected as well. It became submerged and lost and has only recently been brought back to light through research initiated by Prof. S. Sambursky of the Hebrew University in Jerusalem,[71] and Richard Sorabji.[72] What survived of John Philoponos in the West was mainly learned from several of his commentaries, preserved in part by Simplicius, on eleven works of Aristotle.[73] The concept of the contingent was taken up by Boethius who rendered the Greek verb ἐνδέχεται by the Latin *contingit* and gave us the term "contingent", but under the guidance of Aristotelian philosophy and logic it was understood in relation to the concept of συμβεβηκός or the "accidental" on the one hand and to the concept of ἀνάγκη or "necessity" on the other hand, and as such was not regarded as subject to true scientific knowledge. It was in that Boethian way that contingence was understood and used by St Thomas in developing the relations between Christian theology and Aristotelian science. He operated with the classical model of science, *more geometrico,* according to which the object of scientific investigation must be necessary and universal, together with the Aristotelian way of relating matter, form and causality - everything particular, incidental or accidental being excluded from genuine knowledge. However, the Christian doctrine of creation, in accordance with which all creaturely beings are such that they would be non-beings if left to themselves, introduced an ambiguous modification into the Aristotelian way of thinking which affected the notion of contingence. While contingence continued to be defined by reference of effect to cause, the nature of the Supreme Cause, God the Creator, was differently regarded, as was also the way in which contingent things and events depend on him. In creating and sustaining the world, and imposing upon it an all-embracing divine order, God was held to

---

[71] S. Sambursky, *The Physical World of late Antiquity,* London, 1962, pp. 6f, 14f, 74ff. 85ff, 113ff, 151f, 165, 172f, etc.

[72] Richard Sorabji, *Time, Creation and the Continuum,* London, 1983.

[73] See Walter Böhm, *Johannes Philoponos. Ausgewälte Schriften,* München, Paderborn, Wien, 1967.

provide necessary causes for effects which he willed to be necessary; but for effects which he willed to be free God was held to provide what St Thomas called `contingent active causes', i.e. causes which are able to act otherwise.[74] Thus contingent things and events were considered to be related to their cause in such a way that they could be and not be from it. If all things in the world were contingent (that is might not have been) nothing would ever have begun to be, for nothing begins to be except of something that is - a being whose existence is necessary or one which must exist by its nature. If such a necessary and primary reality were to disappear, nothing would remain. Every effect in the world, therefore, must be understood to depend ultimately on God as the First Cause, *Prima Causa*, who transcends and (as the Unmoved Mover) inertially determines the whole cosmic order. So far as contingence is concerned, this means that in the last analysis contingent things and events obtain only under condition of extrinsic relation to what is necessary. That is to say, contingent things and events, while regarded in themselves are baffling and elusive and defy rational knowledge, may be construed in rational discourse only indirectly through being subsumed into relation with a series of necessary relations or reasons terminating on the First Cause. Taken in conjunction with the scientific model, *more geometrico*, which stands for the universal over the particular, the essential over the accidental, and the necessary over the contingent, this had the effect of resolving contingence away in the claim that no scientific knowledge of contingent things and events is possible, not in so far as they are contingent, but only in so far as they may be related to what is necessary. Thus in St Thomas' way of relating science to God whose necessary and timeless being inertially grounds and orders all empirical existence, a necessitation is imparted to it which undermined its distinctively contingent nature. As I understand it, it is a perception of this point that seems to underlie philosophical revolt against traditional and especially Thomist argument from contingence to God who through his necessary and timeless being inertially grounds and orders all empirical existence, thereby imparting to it a hidden determinism which undermines its distinctively empirical nature. It was the Blessed John Duns Scotus rather than St Thomas who advocated an understanding of contingence as it had risen in Greek thought of the first six centuries, but it was the way in which Thomist thought related theology to the hylomorphism of Aristotelian natural philosophy that prevailed.

Of course already in the later middle ages there developed ways of thought which pointed ahead to what we know as empirical science. But to me, the most significant movement for change had to do with the demand for a new kind of question to replace that developed in Medieval scholasticism. This was a demand, however, that came from the Renaissance lawyers rather than the

---

[74] St Thomas, *In Libros perihermeneias Expositio*, 1,14. Cf. also my discussion in *Divine and Contingent Order*, Oxford, 1981, p.86f.

scientists or theologians.[75] I think here above all of Lorenzo Valla of Bologna. What stimulated Valla was not early Christian thinking about the contingent universe and appropriate ways of pursuing knowledge of it, but the kind of open interrogative inquiry pursued in the old Roman Courts of law, of which he read mostly in the works of Cicero (*De inventione, De oratore, Topica*). This deployed what was known as *ars inveniendi*, a `logic of discovery', in which investigators sought to let some reality bear witness to itself in ways appropriate to it and press itself upon their judgment. This called in the first instance, not for logical reasoning, but for a mode of free `topical' or probable reasoning deployed to allow some reality or a state of affairs come to light in its own self-evidence. Valla was impressed with the way in which the Roman jurisconsults interrogated people, events, acts, and circumstances, through subjecting them to question after question, until the truth was forced out into the open when appropriate action could be taken. When Valla directed this *ars inveniendi* to history, it quickly exposed as forgeries the collection of letters from popes and canons of councils, which became known as `the False Decretals'. When *ars inveniendi* in the form of empirical questioning was appropriated and adapted for the investigation of nature by Copernicus and Galileo, and also by Bacon, who had all been trained in Renaissance law, it played a significant role in the development of empirical science.

It was thus that a vast change began to take place in the scientific thinking of the sixteenth and seventeenth centuries, considerably fortified by the renewed attention given during the Reformation to the doctrine of creation out of nothing. This called for a deeper respect for the created order of nature and a deeper understanding of its God-given rationality. It was this that injected a strong empirical ingredient into the foundations of western science which made it possible. However, the old problems remained and in some ways became even more acute. This was largely due to the carry-over of Aristotelian notions of science and causality from the medieval world, and their alignment with the quantification of all observed phenomena and observational data demanded by Galileo. Thus developed, natural science became concerned, not so much with a description of the nature of things themselves or an explanation of things in terms of their intrinsic intelligibility, but with the mathematical organization of observational phenomena and experimental results through deductive geometrical models.

In Newton's great *Principia Mathematica* the system of the world was rigorously thought out through clamping down upon "relative apparent space and time" "absolute mathematical space and time", that is, notions of space and time that are not affected by empirical events. Newton certainly claimed that in the last resort nature itself must tell us how we are to think of it and verify our propositions about it, but his rigid mathematical system had the effect of imposing upon scientific inquiry into phenomenal and empirical processes a way

---

[75] Cf. my account of this in *The Hermeneutics of John Calvin*, Edinburgh, 1988, pp. 100ff.

of thinking about them within a frame of ideal conditions. That in turn gave rise to idealized patterns in the formulation of scientific knowledge in which contingent features and relations in the actual world tended to be rationalized away. The general trend in European thought was set by Descartes, Newton, and Leibniz, who in different ways developed scientific methods of determining regularities discovered in nature and of formalizing understanding of them in necessary universal laws. The movement of thought was steadily from contingence to necessity, or rather from apparent contingence to underlying necessity, which was given massive deterministic form through Kant's transposition of causality from the objective connections which things have externally with one another into regulative and necessary principles of thought, in total disregard of things in themselves, which meant that the laws of nature are not regarded as read out of nature but as imposed by the human mind upon nature.

When the Medieval notion of God as the Unmoved Mover was carried over in the masterful principle of *inertia* into Newtonian physics and mechanics and thought out with reference to absolute space and time and formalized strictly within the necessitarian structure of Euclidean geometry, the concept of contingence was ultimately resolved away, and, although Newton himself denied that the world exists by necessity and by the same necessity follows the laws proposed, there arose the concept of the non-contingent, self-consistent, closed deterministic universe of cause and effect without any ontological reference beyond itself. Certainly attempts were made, mainly through analogical reasoning, to relate the universe of space and time to God as the *Prima Causa*, but the more mathematically rigorous classical physics became, the more the universe was conceived to be a closed non-contingent self-explanatory mechanistic system, such that there was not and could not be anything like a logico-causal bridge between the world and God. Certainly serious attempts were made to retain the concept of contingence, as with Leibniz, but he did little more than reformulate the medieval notion of contingence through his principle of maximum determination in the divine reason for the creation. That is to say, as with Aquinas, contingent events were understood only as they could be considered in a sequential series of events and relations which terminate upon necessary being. Whereas for Leibniz and Aquinas, as of course for Newton, ultimate place was given to God, the closed, necessitarian or determinist structure of the universe increasingly elaborated by classical physics and mechanics inevitably precluded reference to God. Any other way of thinking was ruled out of consideration when the Newtonian system of the world was finally closed upon itself by Kantian metaphysics.

2

Modern science devoted to the investigation of empirical phenomena could not have arisen in the classical form given to it by Galileo and Newton if it had been restricted to a purely *a priori* approach. It arose out of the way of understanding of the universe as created by God and endowed by him with a created or contingent rationality of its own dependent upon his transcendent rationality. By its very nature the concept of contingence could not have arisen from within science itself. As we have seen it arose out of the Judaeo-Christian doctrine of creation out of nothing, and was through the doctrine of the Incarnation. That means, on the one hand, that the contingence of the world cannot be demonstrated from the world itself. As contingent the world is ultimately explainable only from beyond itself, through transfinite reference to God. *Nihil constat de contingentia nisi ex revelatione.* On the other hand, the nature of the contingent universe, created by God as an orderly reality utterly distinct from himself, means that scientific understanding of the universe must be pursued through giving attention to the universe, apart from God, *acsi Deus non daretur*, as Grotius expressed it. And yet - this is the baffling thing about contingence - the independence of the universe from God is itself dependent on God and is sustained by him. That coupling and decoupling of the contingent universe with God lies deep in the foundations of our western science, but the decoupling loses its significance when its relation to the coupling of God and science is neglected or severed, as happened in the Enlightenment, e.g. in the exclusive attention given to the question "how?" and the rejection of the question "why?". That is the problem, as I see it, of the history of empirical science since the seventeenth century. Empirical science rests upon the concept of the contingent nature and order of the universe which does not contain a sufficient explanation within itself, yet it was pursued through the development of self-explanatory modes and systems of thought in the development of non-contingent necessitarian conceptions of the universe, which threatened the very base upon which it rested and had to go on resting as empirico-theoretic science. However, that is not the whole story, for the all-important empirical ingredient in our science, knowledge of things strictly in accordance with their nature, κατὰ φύσιν, kept prompting the development of scientific inquiry into the intrinsic intelligibility of things, and demanding new modes of rational formalization appropriate to them. This is a modern counterpart to the kind of kataphysic (κατὰ φύσιν) heuristic science (εὑρετικὴ ἐπιστήμη) developed by Christian thinkers in the second century to cope with what is quite new and cannot be explained in terms of what is already known. Epistemological and scientific reconstruction of that kind has actually been going on since the middle of the 19th century, with the result that the concept of contingence and contingent rationality has steadily been forcing its way back through the hard crust of necessitarian and determinist thought which overlay it. Thus a fresh way of thinking about the coupling of "God" and "science" has been taking place, which is much more congenial to Christian faith.

What I would like to do now is to point to several areas in the development of science where contingence has increasingly become evident, and where contingent order is found by science to belong to the essential nature of the universe.

It is to James *Clerk Maxwell* that we must turn first.[76] In his account of the of light and electro-magnetism he developed the concept of the continuous dynamic field as a reality in which he broke away from the mechanistic interpretation of nature elaborated in Newton's system of the world. Instead of thinking in terms of particles acting externally on one another he thought of them as continuously and dynamically interrelated and interlocked with one another spreading with a velocity equal to the velocity of light. This called for a way of thinking not analytically from parts to a whole but from a "primitive whole" to constituent parts which led to new experimental facts and required a new mathematical mathesis.[77] This he set out in mathematical equations representing the dynamic structure of the field. According to Einstein the discovery of the mathematical properties of light and the formulation of these differential equations was the most important event in the history of physics since Newton's time, not least because they formed the pattern for a new type of law. In this way Clerk Maxwell probed into a deeper level of intelligibility, disclosing a new reality, a concept for which there was no place in the mechanical description of nature. Thus he began to uncover something of the contingent order that permeates the created universe. Contingent events cannot be treated like random or chance events, for they have a distinctive order of their own but one nevertheless accessible to appropriate mathematical formulation. How are they then to be coordinated with the chains of physical causes formulated in classical physics, and with the concept of a final cause? Causal connections, he argued, have to be looked at on two different levels, a lower level where subordinate centres of causation operate, and a higher level where we have to do with the operation of a *central cause*, the first being treated as a limiting case of the second. In his investigations the scientist, Clerk Maxwell said, has to focus `the glass of theory and screw it up sometimes to one pitch of definition and sometimes to another, so as to see down into the different depths', otherwise everything merges dimly together.[78] Thus through a proper adjustment of the telescope of theory he is enabled to see beyond the subordinate fact of physical acts and their immediate consequences, to the central focus or cause where he is concerned with the original act behind all subordinate causal connections. However, far from thinking of this final cause as the unmoved Mover in the medieval concept of *Prima Causa* or the absolute framework of the Newtonian system, Clerk Maxwell thought of it after the analogy of a *moral* or *personal*

---

[76] James Clerk Maxwell, *A Dynamical Theory of the Electromagnetic Field*, new edition, Edinburgh, 1982, reprinted, Eugene, Oregon, 1996; and see also "Christian Faith and Physical Science in the Thought of James Clerk Maxwell", in my *Transformation and Convergence in the Frame of Knowledge*, Belfast, 1984, pp.215-242.

[77] James Clerk Maxwell, *A Treatise on Electricity and Magnetism*, 3rd ed. vol. 2, London & New York, 1954, pp. 176f.

[78] Cited in Lewis Campbell and William Garnett, *The Life of James Clerk Maxwell*, London, 1882, pp. 236ff.

centre of activity, that is to God the Creator. And he understood this central cause or focus of reference in the light of the dynamic nature of the living God revealed in the incarnation of his Son in Jesus Christ. We shall return to that later, but at this point, all I want to say is that for Clerk Maxwell the contingent nature of the world brought to light in his dynamical theory of the electromagnetic field called for a new and deeper way of coupling thoughts of God and science. We must not overlook here the fact that the finite speed of the propagation of light waves together with the finite speed of electromagnetic waves carried with it an understanding of the universe as finite in nature and extent and thus not as self-sufficient or self-explanatory but as pointing beyond itself altogether. Thus with Clerk Maxwell the notion of contingence, smothered in classical physics and mechanics, broke out once more into the open in a decisive way demanding scientific recognition.

We turn next to *Albert Einstein*,[79] and the epistemological revolution brought about by general relativity theory in the integration of empirical and theoretical, the phenomenal and the mathematical, factors in scientific inquiry. With his comprehensive distinction between absolute and relative, true and apparent, mathematical and common, Newton operated with a radical dualism, in which empirical and theoretical factors were related externally to one another; thus he explained physical features of the world within the rigid framework of Euclidean geometry, that is, a theoretical system of necessary relations independent of time and space. This led to a mechanical, and determinist, close-structured system built up out of static concepts, but it was one which Einstein had been undermined by Clerk Maxwell's concept of the continuous dynamic field. Moreover, with the rise of four-dimensional geometries of space and time, Einstein realized that Euclidean geometry is an idealization, a distorting abstraction of geometry from empirical reality, in which it has been erected into a self-contained conceptual system on its own, pursued as a purely theoretic science antecedent to physics in which we develop our actual knowledge of the world. Rather must geometry be lodged in the heart of physics, where it is pursued as a non-Euclidean geometry in indissoluble unity with physics as the sub-science of its inner rational or epistemological structure and as an essential part of its empirico-theoretical grasp of reality in its objective and intelligible relations. While integrated with space-time reality in this way as a "natural science" geometry remains geometry, but it is not a conceptual system complete in itself, and is consistent as geometry only as it is completed beyond itself in the material content of physics. It is the real geometry of a finite but unbounded universe - the equations of relativity theory predict their own limits. All this implied a rather different view of mathematics which led Einstein, in his 1921

---

[79]   For the following see especially, *The Evolution of Physics, From early concepts to relativity and quanta*, Albert Einstein and Leopold Infeld, New York, 1938; *Ideas and Opinions*, Albert Einstein, New York, 1954; and *The Born-Einstein Letters*, Max Born, London, 1971.

lecture on "Geometry and Experience",[80] to say that if mathematical propositions are certain they are not true, and if they are true they are not certain - by "certain" he referred there to the kind of certainty (necessity) that obtains in Euclidean geometry, and by "true" he referred to what is actually the case in the empirical space-time universe. This implied, of course, that classical logic applies only to flat space, and not to space-time. It was realization of this profound unity between mathematical thinking and the intrinsic intelligibilities of nature that enabled Einstein to resist the pressure to apriorism in his development of relativity theory. While he once had committed himself to say that the task of the physicist is to arrive at those elementary laws from which the cosmos can be built up by pure deduction, he nevertheless went on to insist that experience remains the sole criterion of the physical utility of a mathematical construction. This raises a point to which we must return later, the relation between mathematics embodied in nature and contingent rational order.

Here let me refer to an issue that appears to be particularly significant for our discussion. It concerns the way in which Einstein generalized the role given to light by Clerk Maxwell, attributing to it a unique metaphysical as well as physical status in the universe. In the case of all bodies in motion, motion is defined relationally in terms of space and time, while space and time are defined relationally in terms of light. Light itself, however, is not defined in relation to anything else, for its status is unique: here our science comes to a meaningless stop! Or does it? In a very interesting lecture in 1929 "On the Present State of Field-Theory"[81] - one highly illuminating for our understanding of Einstein himself - he argued that in pressing toward the goal of an ultimate logical uniformity we do not just want to know *how* nature is, but want to know *why nature is what is and not otherwise*. No doubt, he granted, there is a Promethean element lodged in the very concept of logical uniformity which would involve understanding empirical lawfulness as logical necessity even for God! This is an area in scientific reflection, the inner core of nature's secrets, which he found continually fascinating; it is so to speak, he said, *"the religious basis of the scientific enterprise"*. In raising the question *why?* Einstein was asking a question, set aside during the Enlightenment, about the ultimate reason or justification for the laws of nature - that is to say, he realized that far from being self-explanatory, the laws of nature are finally open-structured and are contingent upon an ultimate rational ground of order beyond themselves. In theological terms Einstein's *why?* indicates that natural laws as laws of the contingent universe have a limited validity, and are what they ultimately as *laws* by reference to the commanding and unifying rationality of God the Creator and Sustainer of the universe. It is in that light that I regard Einstein's well-known sayings about God: "God does not play dice". "God does not wear his heart on his sleeve." "God is subtle but not devious." "God does not play tricks with us."

---

[80]   *Ideas and Opinions*, pp. 232-249.

[81]   "Über den Gegenwärtigen Stand der Feld-Theorie", *Festschrift zum 70 Geburtstag von Prof. Dr A. Stodola*, Zürich, 1929, pp. 126-132.

At the outermost boundaries of the universe and at the frontiers of science, he was overcome by a religious awe, which he once expressed thus: "That deeply emotional conviction of the presence of a superior reasoning power, which is revealed in the incomprehensible universe, forms my idea of God." Unlike Clerk Maxwell Einstein did not think of this in a personal way, but his frequent references to "God" or "the Old One", nevertheless indicate something of his appreciation of the open contingent character of the universe and its limitless, and indeed `transcendent', rational order, which was reinforced by his acceptance of the incompleteness theorem of Kurt Gödel which showed, as Bertrand Russell expressed it, that we must think in terms of a series of rational levels that are open to one another upward but are not reducible downward.

It was with *quantum theory* which originated with the work of Planck and Einstein, and developed by Niels Bohr, Werner Heisenberg, Arnold Sommerfeld and Max Born, that the biggest break with the strict causality of classical physics took place, so that the way was opened for a deeper appreciation of contingence through recognition of the elusive non-determinist, and apparently discontinuous, behavior of wave-particles in the sub-atomic structure of nature. Problems remained through a carry-over of older habits of thought, e.g. in the very term "quantum-mechanics", but also in the claim of Niels Bohr that in the last resort quantum theory must be expressed in "classical terms". Moreover, difficulties that have arisen in quantum theory, e.g. over the notion of "hidden variables", and are still unresolved, indicate that the more deeply we penetrate into the rational structures of nature in its sub-atomic levels the more we find that the universe does not contain within itself a sufficient explanation of its order - it is ultimately elusive and inexplicable in a variability that will not be forced into preconceived patterns of our thought. And so we are brought back to the contingent conception of the universe as understandable in the last resort only through reference beyond itself to a transcendent ground of rationality.

As I see it the main issue was pin-pointed by Einstein in his reaction against the idea that nature acts discontinuously so that in abandoning the strict causality of classical physics resort had to be made to a way of accounting for the behavior of sub-quantum particles only through the calculation of statistical probabilities, which has in fact proved remarkably successful empirically. Empirico-theoretical science, as Einstein understood it, is devoted to the apprehension and description of realities themselves, and not merely with the probability of their occurrence, far less just with our observations of their occurrence. In his belief that God does not play dice, belief in universal law and order in a world which objectively exists independent of any theory, Einstein was accused of lapsing back into determinism, but that, I believe, was an unfortunate misunderstanding, for as Wolfgang Pauli showed in a long letter to Max Born, Einstein was a realist, not a determinist. In quantum theory Einstein called for a form of continuous, dynamic relatedness inherent in reality, such as had forced itself upon him in relativity theory, but that meant operating with a rather different and deeper conception of rational order for which both classical causality and a chance-necessity, or an indeterminism-determinism dialectic, were irrelevant. In this case the development of quantum theory required a deep change in the basic structure of scientific thought (such as Clerk Maxwell had to face at an earlier point), a change with which Einstein agreed, as we can see in his critical rejection of the Kantian presuppositions in the thinking of Bohr, Born and Heisenberg in which they coupled quantum phenomena with the human observer. However, the intuitive pressure on his mind for an inner reason for natural laws, would not allow Einstein seriously to entertain the notion of irrational discontinuities in the foundational structure of nature or therefore in scientific explanation of its intrinsic order. In holding that the universe is characterized by a mysterious intelligibility which can be understood only at its comparatively elementary levels, Einstein regarded the intelligible relations and structures immanent in nature as ultimately incomplete or open-ended. He was a realist and not a determinist, and a realist precisely because those intelligible relations and structures are not self-explanatory, but are ultimately although elusively open, which chimed in with his views of *real* mathematical propositions (those embodied in the space-time structure of the world) as true and not certain.

Einstein's realism was reinforced by Gödel's criticism of the closed logical structure of the *Principia Mathematica* of Whitehead and Russell, and his account of the nature of mathematical propositions which, while undecidable or incomplete in themselves, are open to proof or completion beyond themselves.[82] What Einstein called for, then, was the recognition of a deeper level of intelligibility than that with which the quantum theorists of Copenhagen and Göttingen seem satisfied, one which implied a profounder conception of the contingent orderliness of nature. There were hints of this in Heisenberg himself when he insisted that quantum theory expressed realities in nature, and declared that nature as revealed through quantum experiments is found to be so subtle and elusive that it cannot be construed in terms of "the couplet chance and necessity". What is needed is a new heuristic way of penetrating into and disclosing the hidden levels of objective intelligibility upon which the structures of nature rest. Heisenberg also tells us that it was after taking up his violin, and playing sometimes for several weeks on end in order to tune into "the Central Order" (an expression he used for God), that he was able to come up with a mathematics more appropriate to the behavior of quanta. As Heisenberg understood it, the principle he called indeterminacy does not refer to something quite random and arbitrary but to a profound elusive intelligible relation of a contingent kind which requires for its elucidation a different set of operational principles where the law of the excluded middle does not apply. What is required is a dynamic principle of intelligible order, without determinism (such as seems to lurk in the Schrödinger equation), coping with increasing innovation, something like a logic of inhomogeneity (Elsasser's expression), different from the logic of homogeneity employed in classical physics and mechanics. In this case, it might well be said that Heisenberg and Einstein were not so very far apart - they were both trying to grasp something of the subtle order immanent in the dynamic behavior of

---

[82]   Kurt Gödel, *On Formally Undecidable Propositions of Principia Mathematica and Related Systems*, tr. by Bruce Meltzer, Edinburgh 1962.

nature's sub-quantum foundations - i.e. the astonishing but rational flexibility and multivariability of the universe, arising out of the freedom which God has conferred upon it in his creation in contingent reflection of his own!

It is evidently the realist coordination of mathematics in an appropriate way with the structures of the empirical world that discloses the contingent character and nature of its order. Correspondingly, it is the coordination of mathematics in an appropriate way with the contingent nature and order of the universe that discloses the deep levels of intelligible relations embedded in the structures of the empirical world. This calls for a closer consideration of what Eugene Wigner (Michael Polanyi's first student) once called "the Unreasonable Effectiveness of Mathematics in the Natural Sciences."[83]

Mathematicians are, it is claimed, either formalists or realists. In that distinction the formalists regard mathematics as reducible to a strictly logical system of propositions without ontological reference beyond themselves, and realists are, as far as I can see, not really realists but idealists, for the "real" entities to which they hold mathematics to refer are of a Platonic kind - that is, they do not operate with the Judaeo-Christian view that *creatio ex nihilo* applies not only to matter but to rational, including mathematical, *form*, as well as matter. It was that insight which originally gave rise to the conception of the contingent nature of the universe and its rational order upon which all our empirical science ultimately rests. As far as I can see, mathematics is effective in the physical sciences because it belongs to the physical world, and reflects and expresses the patterned intelligibilities embodied in it. That is why, Clerk Maxwell, to the horror of professional mathematicians, could hold that the way in which Michael Faraday made use of his idea of lines of force in coordinating the phenomena of magneto-electric induction showed him to have been in reality a mathematician of a very high order. The mathematics of Michael Faraday was what Clerk Maxwell called of an "embodied" kind. I link this with Einstein's point cited above that if mathematical propositions are certain they are not true, and if they are true they are not certain. In their coordination with the dynamic space-time structure of physical or empirical reality, mathematical propositions share with the universe its open structure - far from being false that belongs to their truth. That is why I cannot but coordinate mathematics and contingence.

I would like now to point to the fact that mathematics rigorously used does not lead to a closed necessitarian or self-explaining system of the world which lends itself to aprioristic thinking, but to an open contingent universe. Whenever mathematics is regarded as intimately correlated with the structures of the empirical universe it operates with open-textured or incomplete symbols, for in rigorous operation it is found to have a reference outside its own system which limits the validity of its formalization. That insight ranges across modern science from Blaise Pascal through Georg Cantor to Kurt Gödel and Alan Turing, but eluded some of the greatest mathematicians of modern times, Karl Gauss and

---

[83]   Eugene Wigner, "The Unreasonable Effectiveness of Mathematics in the Natural Sciences", *Communications on Pure and Applied Mathematics*, vol. iii, 190, pp. 1-14.

David Hilbert. With reference to mathematical proof Pascal pointed out that it is impossible to operate only with explicit definitions, for in defining anything in one set of terms we must tacitly assume other terms that remain undefined; to define them we have to presuppose still other terms, and so on in an endless process. Thus even in the strictest mathematical operations we rely upon informal thought-structures, but these informal structures become known only as we rely upon them in developing formal structures. That was an insight on which Michael Polanyi relied in showing that the premises of science cannot be explicitly formulated but are tacitly held as ultimate beliefs which are not open to logical demonstration.

Let me now refer to the development of set-theory by Georg Cantor, a Jewish Christian mathematician in Halle. He regarded a completed set as an infinite magnitude, but he distinguished it as *transfinite* in contrast to the absolute infinity of God. He held that mathematics has to do with a form of rationality which God has imposed upon both the human mind and the universe. It is created harmony between them that gives the universe its rational unity. Hence mathematical deductions from rational structures in the created universe open the way to further discoveries, yet in such a way that finally they point transfinitely beyond themselves. As Bruce Hedman, the Connecticut mathematician, has pointed out,[84] Cantor produced a classical example of contingent rationality when he drew his distinction between transfinite numbers, which exist in the human mind, and the absolute uncreated infinity, which is beyond all human determination and exists only in the mind of God. Since the universe freely created by God might have been other than it is, no scientific deduction from nature must necessarily be so, for it depends upon a transfinite explanation beyond itself. Hence Cantor accepted the impossibility of analyzing mathematically the entire succession of the transfinite. This implied that every scientific theory is open-ended and always revisable. These views led Cantor, to the dismay of his colleagues in the University of Halle, to reject positivism and determinism, but they carried further the concept of mathematical openness heuristically into the future.

This brings us back to the brilliant work of Kurt Gödel in his famous 1931 essay "On formally undecidable propositions of *Principia Mathematica* and related systems". In that work Whitehead and Russell had tried to transcribe pure mathematics into a completely formalized consistent system of logical notions and relations, and to make tacitly accepted rules of inference and operational theorems entirely explicit. Such a formalization of a system was held to be complete when every true proposition expressible within the system is formally decidable from its axioms. This implies that the truth of propositions expressible

---

[84]   Bruce A. Hedman, "Cantor's Concept of Infinity: Implications of Infinity for Contingence", *Perspectives on Science and Christian Faith*, Ipswich, MA, Volume 45, Number 1, March 1993, pp.8-16. See also "Mathematics, Cosmology, and the Contingent Universe", *Perspectives on Science and Christian Faith*, Volume 41, Number 2, June 1989, pp. 99-103. I am happily indebted to both of these essays.

within the system is relative to the system. In that case the problem arises of having to decide what is an acceptable axiomatic system. The all-important criteria for making such a decision here were held to be: *consistency*, meeting the requirements of the law of non-contradiction, and *completeness*, meeting the requirement of the law of the excluded middle. The classical embodiment of such a system was provided by Whitehead and Russell in *Principia Mathematica,* which was meant to be complete as well as consistent. Gödel showed that this was not the case, by demonstrating that in any formalized system of sufficient richness there are, and must be, certain propositions which are not `decidable' (capable of proof or disproof) within the given system, and therefore that it cannot be decided within the system whether the axioms of the system are consistently or mutually contradictory. Thus he demonstrated the inherent limitation of the axiomatic method in which all arithmetical truths are logically derived from a determinate set of axioms. The consistency of such a formal system, if it is consistent, cannot be demonstrated by a proof within it. If it is consistent it is incomplete. Moreover, in line with Cantor, Gödel showed that the true source of the incompleteness attaching to formal systems of mathematics is to be found in the fact that the formation of ever higher types can be continued into the transfinite. Thus undecidable propositions presented in formal systems become decidable through coordination with higher types. A similar result holds for the axiom system of set theory. This demonstrates that in the last analysis we operate in formal systems with basic concepts and axioms which cannot be completely defined, so that we cannot know what the axioms ultimately mean - their truth and meaning lie ultimately beyond themselves. Thus Gödel brought the insights of Pascal and Cantor about the ultimate openness of mathematical propositions and relations to definite proof.

We must coordinate with Gödel's incompletability theorem with the discovery by Alan Turing of *incomputable* statements.[85] They are incomputable not simply because like mathematical statements in Cantor's transfinite set-theory they require an infinite time to compute, but because they are inherently non-computable. With Cantor we have to do with contingent intelligibilities which finally outstrip the grasp of our minds for they impinge upon them from beyond the created order, from the absolute infinity of God the Creator. As I understand it, Gödel was influenced by Cantor's concept of transfinite relations in set theory, but his incompletability theorem both vindicated Cantor and reinforced his recognition of the transcendent ground of order on which mathematics ultimately relies for its effectiveness in natural science. These developments certainly deal a mortal blow to purely logicist views of mathematics, but from far from undermining mathematics they actually strengthen it and contribute to our understanding of its effectiveness. Let me cite here a statement from John Barrow's 1988 article on "The Mathematical Universe". "If the universe is

---

[85] See the article by John D. Barrow, "The Mathematical Universe. The Orderliness of nature can be expressed mathematically. Why?", *The World and I, Natural Science,* May 1989, pp.306-311.

mathematical in some deep sense, then the mysterious undecidableness demonstrated by Gödel and Turing are part of the fabric of the universe rather than merely products of our minds. They show that even a mathematical universe is more than axioms, more than computation, more than logic - and more than mathematicians can know."

All this has given considerable impetus to the movement of mathematico-scientific thought back to an understanding of the nature and rationality of the universe as open-structured and contingent, thereby restoring to their integrity the very foundations upon which classical and modern science rest. The consistence and completeness theorems of Gödel and the non-computable functions of Turing, apply, of course, not simply to mathematics and mathematical science, but to the whole mathematical universe, understood as open-ended and incomplete, yet as completed beyond itself transfinitely in absolute Infinity. Theologically speaking this brings us back again to the coupling of God and science.

3

In this third part of my address we return to the doctrine of the *Incarnation* of the Logos and Word of God in Jesus Christ. As in him God became man without ceasing to be God, so we think of the Creator himself as having become creature within space and time, yet without ceasing to be the Creator through whom and in whom all things visible and invisible in the universe are ordered and sustained. For Christian theology the Incarnation together with the resurrection constitutes the central axis of our understanding of the universe of space and time, and therefore of the relation of God and science, or science and God. It is the Incarnation of the Son and Word of God in space and time, and his resurrection in space and time, that provide us with the frame for our understanding of the contingent universe, in relation to the ultimate source and uncreated ground of all *order*, natural, moral, aesthetic and personal.

As we have noted, it was through the Christian doctrine of the incarnation that the Judaic conception of *creatio ex nihilo* was in such a way that it gave rise to the all-important understanding of the contingent nature and rational order of the universe, which laid the basis for the rise and development of empirical science. However, there took place in the rise of classical physics a steady mathematical formalization of physical law through generalization of scientific observations, so that the laws of nature were held to obtain only under conditions of logical necessity, which had the effect of cutting them off from the contingent basis upon which natural science rest. On the other hand, in the steady penetration of scientific inquiry more and more deeply into the hidden levels of intelligibility upon which all natural order rests, it has become evident that physical law is to be regarded as obtaining only under conditions of contingency in the space-time universe. Since it was the doctrine of the Incarnation that gave rise to the concept of contingence which natural science of itself could not have done, we must ask whether Christian belief can once again make important contributions to natural science which natural science by itself could not make, as in the basic concept of contingence. And here we turn to the point stressed by St Paul that in view of the incarnation and resurrection of the eternal Son of God in Jesus Christ, we must think of all visible and invisible realities in the created cosmos as sustained, conserved and reconciled by him and in him. That is, not simply by and in him as the eternal Creator Word of God but as the Creator Word of God *incarnate in space and time*, and receptively triumphant over all evil and disorder. And this means, if we are to return to the old terms *causa* and *prima causa*, that with the devout James Clerk Maxwell we must think of this ultimately in moral or personal terms, and screw up the telescope of theory to discern the implications of what that means in the intelligible depths of the natural order. There we have an agenda which I believe it is up to us Christians concerned with God and science to pursue in the modern world. But we must give realist attention to incarnation and resurrection of Jesus Christ, God himself with us as one of us. What I wish to do now is to touch upon certain areas at the conceptual and epistemological interface in the God-Science dialogue to which we may give some attention.

Here let us consider again the coordination of mathematics and physical science, to which Wigner gave expression in the memorable words we have already cited about "the unreasonable effectiveness of mathematics in the natural sciences". When we think of this from the perspective of the incarnate Creator, that coordination is not unreasonable but reasonable, for in Christ the created world of space and time is correlated to the ultimate rational ground and to the endless possibilities of the Creator. This explains why nature is endowed with the kind of rational order that constantly surprises us in its manifestation of unexpected features and structures which could not be deduced from what is already known. They are features and structures, however, which nevertheless always turn out to be consistent with other features and structures already known, although these may become modified as limiting cases of new discoveries in much the same way that classical physics is related to relativity physics. What else is this but a manifestation of the contingent intelligibility of the created order, and its objective reality over which we have no control? We have to do here with the astonishing flexibility and multivariability of the universe arising out of the correlation of the contingent freedom of the created order with the transcendent freedom of the Creator. That is the ground of the reasonable effectiveness of mathematics in the natural sciences, but it reverses the classical approach to physical law, and, as I indicated above, means that physical law obtains only under conditions of contingency in the universe. That is to say, physical laws are to be formulated under conditions of contingence, where contingence is held not just as an essential presupposition but as a constitutive factor in the rational structure of all physical law. Thus physical laws, rightly understood, are themselves finally contingent. What we need, therefore, is a "new *mathesis*" in mathematics (to use Clerk Maxwell's expression) in which we understand it in a realist way as deriving from and bound up with the *contingent* character of the rational order of the universe sustained and held together by the incarnate Creator. Let the development of that kind of mathematics be on our Christian agenda.

In giving attention to the Incarnation of the Creator within the created order, we must give serious consideration to the fact that the creative Centre in the universe, the *Causa Prima* of all things in space and time is *personal*, and allow that to affect our understanding of the nature and operation of physical law. This was a point to which the St Basil in the early Church gave attention, in light of the fact that it was through Jesus Christ the incarnate Logos of God that all things were made from nothing and are sustained by him in their order and being. Basil held that the created cosmos is intrinsically *incomplete* - far from being self-sufficient or self-explanatory, it is properly to be understood only as it is contingent upon God, and as given its rational order through the Word of God. All the laws of nature, all its intelligible order, are to be understood as echoing the mighty Word of God. Thus with reference to the Genesis account of creation, he wrote that it was the commanding Voice of God that brought the world into being, and gave rise to the laws of nature. To use another modern expression, it is the Word of God in creation and providence that really constitutes "the cosmological constant". The point I wish to note here has to do with the *personal activity of God* revealed in the Incarnation, which we need to take into account in our God-Science dialogue.

Let me indicate what I mean with reference to a difficulty discussed by John Archibald Wheeler, which arises at zero points where physical laws become critical.[86] That is a baffling problem faced by quantum physics, when it penetrates into the untouchable interior of an elementary quantum phenomenon which Wheeler could speak of as "the act of creation"! There at the frontiers of knowledge where being bounds upon non-being, everything becomes "higgledy-piggledy", and appears lawless or without rational form, but there, Wheeler insists, there must be some deep and simple "*regulating principle*", some "*law apart from law*", that gives order and law to what would otherwise be disorderly and lawless. He believes that the discovery and proper formulation of this "principle" or "law" is the number one task of the coming third era of physics. In his search for this regulating principle Wheeler turns to the patterns of thermodynamics and statistical mechanics for his operative clue, but does not evidently find what he wants. There is and cannot be any logical or computable relation across the gap between being and non-being. My question to him is whether he should not rather give attention to a *non-computable* creative relation, and to *contingent order*, the kind of order that is what it precisely is through being grounded beyond itself, an open-structured form that is consistent only as it is completed beyond itself in meta-reference to a transcendent ground of order. That is, in a way, what Wheeler himself is after in his master-idea that the third era of physics is "recognition-physics" or "meaning-physics" (prompted, I think, by the statement of Steven Weinberg in his book, "The First Three Minutes",

[86]   John A. Wheeler, *Oersted Lecture*, "On recognizing `Law Without Law', *The American Physical Society*, Jan. 15, 1983. For the following see my discussion in *The Christian Frame of Mind, Reason, Order and Openness in Theology and Natural Science,* Colorado, 1989, pp. 55ff, 95ff & 118f.

when he asserts that everything is finally pointless). What Wheeler implies is that physics has reached the point where some sort of *why?* is needed in physics - that is, a *semantic* reference to a meaningful ground beyond itself. My suggestion to John Wheeler is that instead of trying to cross the boundary between being and non-being where disorder appears to arise, through an extension of normal scientific conceptualization or an extrapolation of physical laws, we should come at the problem *the other way round*, not from the physical world to what is beyond, but from God the creative source of all being who has provided the space-time universe with its orderly structures and their initial conditions upon which all scientific inquiry rests. Thus I hope we may find some way of allowing the patterns of God's creative ordering, discerned through his self-revelation in the Incarnation of his Word, to penetrate into the patterns of the contingent universe that become disclosed to scientific inquiry, in the hope of grasping a *new form of order*. It would be at such an intersection of divine and contingent symmetries that the regulating principle, the law apart from law, which Wheeler seeks, may well become disclosed.

That is the sort of endeavor in which, I believe, we ought to be engaged in deep conceptual and epistemological dialogue between theology and science, but it will involve the projection of new forms of thought such as time-related mathematics and logic. Certainly, when we think of reasonable effectiveness of mathematics in the natural sciences as an expression of the contingent order of the space-time universe, we must surely think out the relation of mathematics to *time* and not just to space, as seems to be demanded in a mathematics of the continuous dynamic field.

This brings me to the problem of trying to understand an essentially *dynamic*, continuously expanding, universe through the deployment of static timeless concepts in mathematics and logic - which seems to me to lie, in part at least, behind some of the difficulties arising in so-called "chaos theory". That was a problem bequeathed to science through the Newtonian System of the world conceived in terms of the static absolutes of space and time, which was only partially overcome through the relativistic understanding of space-time, where time still remains an external operator, for the dualism between particle and field has not been entirely resolved away, as Einstein hoped. Attempts have now been made, however, to bring what Henri Bergson called "real time" (not "imaginary time", as Steven Hawking would have it!) into the central focus of scientific inquiry.

I think here particularly of the work of Ilya Prigogine and his collaborators in their account of non-equilibrium thermodynamics, which has led them to develop dynamic notions of being as becoming, and to speak of "the redemption of time" in the emergence of richer patterns of order arising spontaneously upon the random or disorderly fluctuations that occur far from a state of equilibrium. To express this they have put forward mathematical equations for the passage of thought between dynamic and thermodynamic states of matter, but even here, as far as I am able to judge, while time is brought as an internal operator into physics, it is still not built into the warp and woof of mathematics. What we need is a radically new mathesis of dynamical reasoning in mathematics, such as Clerk

Maxwell indicated but died too soon to develop, in which real time relations belong to and operate within the basic structures of mathematics. Certainly, as Edward Nelson the distinguished Professor of Mathematics in Princeton has said, we have yet to enter fully into the revolutionary implications of Clerk Maxwell's concept of the continuous dynamic field.

Similarly what we need is something like a *logic of verbs* in which time is built as an essential factor into the inner process of logical reasoning - as far as I am aware, the nearest that has been produced in this respect is the work on *tense logic* by the late A. N. Prior. His work took its rise from a discussion in which some of us were involved in Oxford in 1939, when we discussed the problem set by Kierkegaard on how to do justice to the notion of "becoming" in the Johannine statement "the Word *became* flesh". That requires a dynamic mode of thought appropriate to the movement of the Word in *becoming* flesh in space and time. No theologian has advanced thought further along this line than Karl Barth in his way of integrating being and act and act and being in his doctrine of God, and thus of God's becoming flesh as the living movement of his being. What he taught has not been properly grasped by people who cannot think about God's becoming except in some sort of Aristotelian or Hegelian way of being as preceding becoming and of becoming as passing over into something else. What we require today in theology and in science are new subtle modes of thought, to which I believe Christian minds governed by the truth of the Incarnation and Resurrection ought to give themselves.

Christians must reflect much more profoundly and realistically about the implications of the Incarnation, of God the Creator himself, God personally incarnate in space and time. God's coming among us and as one of us was an utterly astonishing event, something quite new, not only for the created order, but even for God who was not always incarnate, as he was not always Creator. What are the implications of the incarnation in space and time, of God incarnate in space and time once for all, for our understanding of space and time? And what are the cognate implications of the Resurrection and Pentecost, events that were also new even for God? Certainly it means that we must give closer attention to the view of Clerk Maxwell that since the universe created by God is essentially one, there are fundamental affinities between the laws of the external world of space and time and the laws of the human mind. Hence although physics does not and cannot mediate to us knowledge of other truths it may well supply us with "real analogies" (Clerk Maxwell's expression) which we may use to help articulate knowledge we reach on other ground. I think here, for example, of the way in which our understanding of the unique physical and metaphysical status of light as the universal "constant" in the universe may help us to think out and articulate the bearing of the faithfulness of God upon all things invisible and visible. It was indeed through the distinction between uncreated light and created light that John Philoponos was led to develop his physics of light and to overthrow Platonic and Aristotelian notions of the eternity of the world. But what of fresh and deeper understanding of *time* which we may gain from thinking out the distinction between uncreated time, the time of the eternal life of God, and created time, the time of the contingent order? May conceptual and epistemological dialogue between theology and natural science not help us here to deepen our understanding of the physical world of space and time? I think here once again of the way in which Clerk Maxwell developed his physical and dynamical mode of reasoning about how light particles interrelate internally with one another in a continuous dynamic field, when the Christian doctrine of inter-personal relations in God was allowed to exercise a regulative role in his formation of scientific theory - that was an ontological and epistemological development which altered the rational structure of physics. Let me emphasize that Clerk Maxwell did not inject theological concepts as such into his dynamical theory of the electromagnetic field, but he did allow deep Christian convictions to exercise a regulative role in his scientific judgment and choice of concept and theory. If that happened at a supreme juncture in the advance of physical science, why may this not happen again, especially when we think out the implications of the incarnate advent of the Creator himself into space and time, not least in helping scientific inquiry to penetrate into and find adequate expression for the subtle and flexible modes of connection in created reality? I myself believe that a profound and rigorous grasp of the Christian doctrines of the Incarnation and Resurrection in thinking out the relations of God and science today may make a real break-through, not least in helping natural science to reach something like the regulative principle or law apart from or beyond law which it cannot achieve on its own.

Chapter 5

Science and Access to God: Epistemological Perspective

1

Access to God and access to science considered together, access to scientific understanding of the creation and access to theological understanding of God, go back to the great theologians and scientists of Alexandria in the first six centuries of the Christian era. There already shortly before the first century there arose scientists who were dissatisfied with trying to understand the world in *a priori* abstract theoretical forms in Platonic, Aristotelian or Stoic ways, and set about developing a new kind of open inquiry in which they asked positive questions or framed "thought experiments" designed to disclose the nature of the realities into which they inquired. These natural scientists or φυσικοί were sharply criticized by skeptical thinkers of the New Academy like Sextus Empiricus who called them the δογματικοί or "dogmatics", not because they were dogmatic in the later sense of that word, but because they were concerned to ask questions that might yield true answers under the positive or dogmatic constraint of nature.[87] They regarded science as proceeding strictly in accordance with nature, κατὰ φύσιν, in order to disclose the actual nature of any reality in question. This was called δογματικὴ ἐπιστήμη or "dogmatic science" in which scientific thinking κατὰ φύσιν was pursued faithfully under the constraint of what the nature of something really is, κατ' ἀληθείαν, and allowed the conceptual assent (πίστις) of our minds to that reality, as it becomes progressively disclosed to us, to determine how we are to think truly of it and express our understanding of it. In this context the terms φύσις and ἀλήθεια, nature and reality, were equivalent. This rigorous scientific mode of inquiry (ἡ μέθοδος τῆς εὑρέσεως) was held to apply to every field of scientific knowledge, when an appropriate modality of the reason was developed under the constraint of the specific nature of the object and the information it yielded.

In Alexandria that was how scientific theological inquiry concerned with the nature and activity of God was regarded and developed by the great theologians

---

[87]   Sextus Empiricus, *Adversus Dogmatikos*, I, viii-xxix.

of the ancient Church.[88] They too, especially Cyril of Alexandria, spoke of Christian theology as ἐπιστήμη δογματική, or "dogmatic science", in which they allowed the nature of God, as he has revealed himself to mankind through the reality of his incarnate Word, to govern how they were to think out and give rigorous expression to its truth in faithful conformity to it, that is strictly κατὰ φύσιν and κατ' ἀληθείαν θεοῦ. In the course of that development of dogmatic science, it was understandable that theologians and scientists, θεολογοί and φυσικοί, should influence each other. That is my concern here, with the way in which access to God through his self-revelation affected access to natural science, and thus in which access of theological science to creation affected access of natural science to God. It was such a movement of thought that took place, when the Fathers of the Church hammered out their basic forms of thought and speech, not only in the literary and philosophical culture of the day, but in the midst of the most advanced scientific achievements of the ancient world.

It was in Alexandria particularly that theological and scientific traditions flowed together, and theology and science interacted with each other conceptually, epistemologically and linguistically. Owing to the fact that immense attention was devoted to the doctrines of the incarnation and creation, and of the incarnation within the created order of space and time, a radical transformation in the foundations of knowledge and in cosmological outlook took place: theology and science began to be pursued together within the same unitary world of space and time so that careful attention had to be given to the whole created order as it came from God and as it is sustained by his Word or Λόγος. It is above all, I believe, to John Philoponos of Alexandria in the sixth century,[89] theologian and physicist, that we must turn if we are to grasp best something of how knowledge of God and knowledge of the cosmos interacted with each other in a very fruitful and utterly astonishing way, one in which, as we now know, the ultimate foundation upon which all modern empirico-theoretical science was laid. It is on that ground, I believe, that we may understand how access to God and access to science belong together, and how we may with appropriate reserve speak of science in our day as opening and serving access to God.

Already Christian theologians like Athanasius, Basil and Cyril had begun to think out the Christian understanding of God and the world in ways which John Philoponos had revolutionary implications for classical philosophy and science. Three basic points may be noted. (a) The biblical doctrine of the one God, the Creator of all things visible and invisible, called in question Greek polytheism and pluralism, polymorphism, hylomorphism and dualism, and demanded a unitary view of the created universe which required a scientific way of knowing

---

[88] See my account of this scientific method in "The Hermeneutics of Clement of Alexandria", *Divine Meaning*, 1994, pp. 130-178.

[89] See *The Physical World of Late Antiquity*, by Samuel Sambursky, 1962, and *Philoponus and the rejection of Aristotelian science,* edit. by Richard Sorabji, 1987, and John McKenna, *The Life-Setting of The Arbiter of John Philoponos*, 1997.

that answered to its rational order. (b) The biblical view of the goodness of the creation, reinforced by the doctrine of the incarnation of the eternal Logos or Son of God within the creation, destroyed the idea that sensible and empirical events are not accessible to rational thought, and established instead the reality of the empirical world in the recognition that temporal and sensible realities have a common rationality of a contingent (ἐνδεχόμενος) kind, open to scientific investigation and understanding. (c) The fact that God himself, in creating the universe out of nothing, has conferred upon it one comprehensive rational order, dependent on his own, had the effect of destroying the Aristotelian and Ptolemaic separation between the sensible and the intelligible worlds, and so between terrestrial and celestial mechanics, and at the same time gave rise to dynamic and relational concepts of space and time as bearers of rational order in the created universe. That was the Christian view of God and the created universe which John Philoponos inherited and set out to develop and defend against Neoplatonic and Aristotelian attacks, and on that basis to deepen and develop scientific and theological understanding of the created order.

Reflection on two major ingredients in this theological inheritance opened up for Philoponos a revolutionary conception of natural science, which then fed back into his incarnational theology giving it a more realist and dynamic emphasis not least in respect of the understanding of space and time. These were: (1) the demand of the Judaeo-Christian doctrine of *creatio ex nihilo* for a radical rethinking of the classical Greek conceptions of the universe; and (2) the bearing of the distinction between *uncreated and created light* upon the classical sciences of optics, physics and dynamics. Both of these had the effect of generating a scientific outlook upon the created order that was congenial and conducive to doctrinal formulation of Christian Faith.

(1) The Christian doctrine of creation understood from the perspective of the incarnation of God the Word in space and time.

It was in Alexandria, the great centre where classical science and cosmology had reached its height, but where a stultifying amalgam of Aristotelian and Neoplatonic ideas had come to prevail under the teaching of Proclus, that John Philoponos opened his attack upon the pagan ideas of the eternity of the world in his work *De aeternitate mundi contra Proclum*, and followed it up by *De aeternitate mundi contra Aristotelem* developed in a series of critical commentaries on the works of Aristotle.[90] In them he set out a philosophico-scientific account of the Christian doctrine of creation out of nothing, and of the unitary universe with a rejection of epistemological and cosmological dualism which he claimed obstructed scientific investigation of empirical and cosmological realities. He demolished Aristotle's notion of the "aither" or the so-

---

[90]   Preserved by Simplicius in *Commentaria in Aristotelem graeca*, vols. 13-17, ed. by H. Diels, Berlin, 1882-1909. See also *Philoponus Against Aristotle on the Eternity of the World*, tr. by C. Wildberg, 1987.

called "fifth element",[91] and with it the myth of eternal cycles and unending time,[92] and throughout advanced a powerful account of the open-structured nature of the universe as freely created by God and endowed with a contingent rational order of its own. Of particular importance for Philoponos was the idea that God created both matter and form out of nothing, and created it in a non-temporal way, while creating time itself along with the world.[93]

Added to these critical scientific and epistemological arguments against Neoplatonists and Aristotelians, John Philoponos offered a more positive account of the Christian doctrine of creation, in the *De opificio mundi*.[94] In it he had in mind St Basil's *Homilies on the Hexaemeron*,[95] but throughout he was concerned to give scientific expression to the biblical doctrine of creation. Here it becomes clear that it was his distinctively Christian understanding of creation that had opened up for Philoponos the possibility of a genuinely scientific account of the world of space and time, freeing it from the philosophical myths of the Greeks. Here also we see that it was his theological understanding of the contingent rational order of the universe of space and time free from necessity that provided him with access to the actual nature of the universe, and helped him to put forward a genuine scientific understanding of the empirical laws of its order.

(2) The theological distinction between uncreated and created light.

The understanding of God as Light, not just in a symbolic sense, was a primary element in the teaching of Athanasius about God as Creator and Logos: God *is* Light.[96] Due largely to the teaching of St John light had early become a primary element in Christian thought in worship and theology alike, particularly as identified with Christ.[97] Like St Basil in his *Homilies on the Hexaemeron*, John Philoponos gave attention to the Biblical account in the Book of Genesis of creation through the majestic fiat of God, including the creation of light: "Let there be light, and there was light." And he distinguished this created light from

---

[91] Cf. Aristotle, *De caelo*, 1; and Philoponos, *Contra Proclum* (edit. by H. Rabe, 1899), XIII, 485-491.

[92] 6Cf. Aristotle, *Physica*, 8.1; Philoponos, *In physica*, *Fragment* 108, & *Con. Proclum*, I.6-8, XI.12.

[93] Philoponos, *In Physica*, 189, & *Fragment* 73; *In De Caelo*, 136-138; *In Physica*, *Fragment*, 108-126 & 132; cf. Christian Wildberg, *Philoponus Against Aristotle on the Eternity of the World*, 1987. pp. 122ff, 128ff.

[94] Edit. by G. Reichardt, Leipzig, 1897.

[95] See my account of this in *The Christian Frame of Mind*, 1989, pp. 1-6.

[96] See, for example, *De decretis*,27, & *Ad Serapionem*,1.19.

[97] See for example the great hymn Φῶς ἱλαρόν attributed to Gregory the Theologian of Nazianzus.

the uncreated light of the divine Logos.[98] That was a distinction, similar to that between creative Spirit and created spirit, which became all-important for Philoponos,[99] for it exercised a major role not only in his theology but in his science, and not only in optics, but in dynamics. It had the effect of reinforcing his rejection of the radical dualism in Hellenic philosophy and science between visible and invisible, tangible and intangible realities, and thus between terrestrial and celestial mechanics. All this called in particular for fresh thinking about the physics of light which he undertook in controversial examination of the teaching of Aristotle, especially as expressed in the *De anima*,[100] which opened the door for something like a dynamic field theory (ἕξις τις) of light.[101]

In contrast to Aristotle's static notion of light Philoponos put forward a conception of light as a real activity. Thus he spoke of light as an immaterial or incorporeal dynamic force (κινητική τις δύναμις ἀσώματος, ἐνέργειά τις ἀσώματος κινητική), invisible in a medium like air, which moves directionally and continuously at a timeless or unlimited velocity.[102] As Philoponos wrote in his work against Proclus, the movement or speed of light is so fast that it can be said to be timeless (ταχεῖα...ἢ ἄχρονος).[103]

This concept of light as incorporeal kinetic activity, which Philoponos called φωστικὴ δύναμις,[104] had far-reaching implications for optics, physics and dynamics: it involved a new kinetic theory, in sharp antithesis to that of Aristotle. What Philoponos did, taking his cue from the kinetic propagation of light, was in fact to propound a new theory of impetus (κινητικήν τινα δύναμιν ἀσώματον) on the analogy between the impetus imparted to a projectile in being hurled and the incorporeal kinetic force or momentum in the movement of light imparted to it by the Creator. Philoponos' light theory and impetus theory together amounted to a radical rejection of Aristotelian physics and mechanics and registered an immense advance in scientific understanding of the universe, approaching that of modern times. This combination of light theory and impetus theory was congenial, as Philoponos realized, to the Christian doctrine of creation out of nothing, for God himself is the creative source of all matter and form, and all

---

[98] Basil, *Hexaemeron*, VI.2. This was a distinction also found in the West as with St Augustine, *Con. Faustum Manichaeum*, 20.7.

[99] *De Opificio mundi*, edit. by W. Reichardt, 1897, Or. II & III, and cf. p. 10, 74f, & 76ff. See also John McKenna, op.cit. Ch. 3, pp. 93ff.

[100] See Samuel Sambursky, *The Physical World of late Antiquity*, 1962, pp. 110ff; Walter Böhm, *Johannes Philoponos*, 1978, pp. 139ff, 182ff & 188ff; and Richard Sorabji, *Philoponos and the rejection of Aristotelian Science*, 1987, pp. 26ff.

[101] See Philoponos, *In De anima*, 438 b & 430 a. Cf. Böhm, op. cit. pp.176f, 188ff, 195 & 308.

[102] See Böhm, op.cit. pp. 1185, 187f, 315f & 445; cf. also Sambursky, op.cit., p. 115.

[103] *De aeternitate mundi contra Proclum*, 1.8.22.

[104] *De aeternitate mundi contra Proclum*, I.8.22.

light and energy in the universe.[105] Thus for Philoponos light theory and impetus theory together scientifically reinforced and contributed to the unitary view of heaven and earth, matter and form, space and time, freely created by God Almighty out of nothing, for it was through the eternal Word or Logos incarnate in Jesus Christ, the Light of the world, that he has freely endowed them with their active force (κινητικὴ δύναμις) and continues to maintain and hold them together in their rational order.

The combination of Philoponos' dynamic and relational theories of light and motion reinforced the open-structured notions of space and time already developed by theologians, and gave rise to a conception of the universe as governed throughout by an internal cohesion (ἕξις) affecting and unifying all activity within it.[106] Thus light theory and impetus theory constituted together a kind of dynamic field theory,[107] anticipating that of James Clerk Maxwell in the nineteenth century. The immediate effect of this in the fifth century was to liberate science from the closed world of Aristotle, nowhere more apparent than in his quantitative notion of space as the immobile limit within which a body is contained,[108] and to replace it with a unified open-structured kind of rational order. The change in the conception of space applies, *mutatis mutandis*, also to Philoponos' relational conception of time in the reciprocal bearing of time and motion upon one another. All this had the effect of profoundly altering the fundamental conception of the nature (φύσις) of things, and consequently of the understanding of scientific inquiry as pursued strictly "in accordance with the nature (κατὰ φύσιν) of things", that is, in accordance with what things really or actually are (κατ' ἀλήθειαν), and therefore in accordance with their dynamic nature or natural force (κατὰ τὴν φυσικὴν δύναμιν). This change toward a radically dynamic and relational conception of the inherent order and nature of the universe carried with it a basic change in the pursuit of objective scientific inquiry itself and correspondingly in the precise meaning and handling of scientific terms. That was nowhere more apparent than in the dynamic conception and meaning of "nature" or φύσις itself, and of "reality" or ἀλήθεια, e.g. in their frequent synonymous relation to one another.[109]

We must not overlook the fact that already in the course of Alexandrian theology, particularly through Athanasius and Cyril, there had come about a steady development in the use of theological terms. Thus in their actual use φύσις, οὐσία, ὑπόστασις, πρόσωπον, had already been stretched, changed, and

---

[105] Philoponos, *In de anima*, 330, 21 & 428 b 9.

[106] For the use of ἕξις in this way see Philoponos *In De anima*, 418b & 430a; and cf. W. Böhm, op. cit., pp. 195 & 308.

[107] Cf. again John McKenna, op.cit, pp. 96ff.

[108] I have discussed this in *Space, Time and Incarnation*, 1969 & 1997, pp. 1-21, and in *Divine Meaning*, 1995, pp. 343-373.

[109] See Samuel Sambursky, *The Physical World of Late Antiquity,* 1962, p. 96f.

developed under the dynamic impact of the Gospel, so that attention must be given to their actual use in particular contexts rather than to their classical Greek definitions. It was in line with that on-going conceptual, epistemological, and linguistic activity that the changes in the scientific use of terms under Philoponos took place, but the results of his scientific revolution had a feed-back upon Christian theology, giving it a more realist and dynamic slant especially in the Alexandrian tradition which, I fear, the West has not properly appreciated. That change is nowhere more important than in the use by John Philoponos of the expression μία φύσις to speak of the μία ἀλήθεια of the incarnate Son of God. It was because that was not recognized or understood by the Aristotelian establishment in Byzantium that Philoponos was condemned and then anathematized as a monophysite heretic, which had the disastrous effect of condemning and rejecting his revolution in natural science, resulting in its loss for many, many centuries. In fact it was not until the revolutionary change that started with the work of James Clerk Maxwell in the combination of light theory and impetus theory that our modern empirico-theoretical science actually arose.

My concern here is not to pursue that further but to discuss the fruitful way in which through John Philoponos, theologian and physicist, Christian theology and natural science can bear fruitfully upon one another. John Philoponos did not intrude his theology upon his science, or his science upon his theology. However, his theological grasp of divine truth opened his eyes to a more realistic understanding of the contingent nature of the world and its distinctive rational order, and exercised a regulative role in his choice and formation of scientific concepts and theories and their explanatory development. At the same time the dynamic character of his physical science, as it arose in this way, had a bearing upon the dynamic character of his theology, and deepened his grasp of its epistemological ground and perspective.

He never thought of arguing from the world to the Creator, for that would have presupposed a logically necessary relation between them, No, he regarded the world as created freely by God and endowed with a contingent form of rationality different from God's transcendent Rationality, but as such pointing openly beyond itself to the Creator. That is to say, his Christian theology opened up for him access to science, and his science thus understood opened up for him access to God. It was the theological distinction between the uncreated Light of God and the created light of the world that was all-important for him. It impelled him to develop the physics of light in a dynamic open-structured way, which radically changed the foundations of ancient science. In so doing John Philoponos anticipated the kind of empirico-theoretical science in which we engage today on the foundation laid down by James Clerk Maxwell when he brought light theory and impetus theory together in his epoch-making work *A Dynamical Theory of the Electromagnetic field.*[110] It was his concept of the

---

[110] Refer to my edition of this work in 1982, reprinted in 1997; and to my account of his thought in *Transformation and Convergence in the Frame of Knowledge*, 1984, ch. 6, pp. 215-242; in *Senso del divino e scienza moderna*, tr. by G. Del Re, 1992, pp. 317-352; and in *Das Verhältnis zwischen christlichem Glauben und moderner*

continuous dynamic field that Einstein hailed as the greatest change in the rational structure of science.[111] What lay behind that change, however, which Einstein did not realize, was Clerk Maxwell's adaptation to physics of the kind of onto-relations expressed in the Christian doctrine of the Holy Trinity, in which the relations between the three divine Persons belong to what they really are.[112] That way of thinking out in a non-necessary, non-mechanical, and non-logical way, the dynamic relations of light particles with one another in the magnetic field, revealed the kind of access which Christian theology can have to natural science, and thereby also revealed the kind of access on *epistemological grounds* that natural science can have for Christian theology. It is, I believe, in this epistemological perspective, in which we engage in the conceptual interface of theological and natural science, that we may rightly ask questions about the way in which natural science, pursued in this dynamic relational way hand in hand with theology, can open for us today a mode of access to God.

2

In the rest of this address I want to discuss the way in which we may consider the kind of access which natural science in relation to theological science may be said to serve access to God. Theologians and scientists live and work within the same empirical world of space and time, which both theologians and scientists have to take seriously, when there is inevitably an overlap in their inquiries, and in the modalities of the reason which they develop under pressure from the different realities with they have to do. How then, in our modern era, may we think of the access of natural science to God?

Of massive significance, of course, is the concept of *contingence*, contingent reality and contingent order,[113] upon which all our modern science, particularly since Clerk Maxwell and Einstein, is based.[114] As we have already noted it was the Biblical concept of *creatio ex nihilo* by Christian theology that made empirical science rationally possible and indeed gave rise to its early beginnings. By contingence is meant that the whole universe of matter and form was freely created by God and endowed with a rationality of its own utterly distinct from

---

Naturwissenschaft. Die geistesgeschichtliche Bedeutung von James Clerk Maxwell,1982.

[111] Albert Einstein, Leopold Infeld, *The Evolution of Physics,* 1938, "Field, Relativity", pp. 125 ff; also, Einstein, *The World as I See it*, pp. 156-161; and Einstein's appreciation of Clerk Maxwell, pp.29-32, in my edition of *A Dynamical Theory of the Electromagnetic Field.*

[112] For that he was evidently indebted to Robert Boyd, *Praelectiones in Ephesios*, 1661, cc. 487 et seq.

[113] I have discussed this at length in *Divine and Contingent Order*, 1981 & 1998.

[114] Refer to my contribution to *John Paul II On Science and Religion. Reflections on the New View from Rome*, 1990, pp. 105ff.

the transcendent rationality of God, but dependent or contingent on it. It is a serious error to think of contingence as chance or to equate the contingent with the accidental, but that is what is often being put forward today by scientists, especially in the field of biology. Appeal to chance is a way not to think, but contingence refers to a positive form of rational order which is not self-explicable but points beyond itself to a transcendent ground of order as the ultimate reason for what it is. In the nature of the case contingence is not something that natural science could ever have come up with and cannot explain - and yet all our natural science and the laws of nature which it seeks to formulate have to do with the intrinsically contingent nature of the universe and its contingent form of rationality. This means that natural science cannot explain itself, and that there is no way of arguing from the contingent nature or rationality of the world explored by science to God, for that would presuppose that the world is not contingent but necessary. It cannot be said, therefore, that natural science or the world of nature which it explores and seeks to comprehend, actually gives us access to God. However, because the world is contingent in its rational order, by its very nature it points openly beyond itself, and cries out, so to speak, mutely for the Creator. Far from closing access to God natural science is an open door to a way of knowing God beyond itself. By the very nature of its contingent rational order, natural science reaches out in its formulation of the laws of nature beyond the boundary of being with non-being, in a tacit semantic reference to some form of "law beyond law", to an ultimate *why* or a *transcendent reason* for the laws which it formulates. In virtue of its contingent nature the world is not finally understandable without relation to God.

That was the issue raised by Albert Einstein in his remarkable lecture in Zürich in 1929 on the present state of field theory, when he claimed that science has now reached the point where we cannot remain satisfied with knowing *how* nature is, and *how* its laws operate, for we want to know *why* nature is what it is and not otherwise (*warum die Natur so und nicht anders ist*). He went on to say that to aim at a "logical uniformity" somehow related to God would be a "promethean" undertaking, but here nevertheless science has to do with the "religious basis" of its scientific struggle (*die religiöse Basis des wissenschaftlichen Bemühens*).[115] That is to say, there is no way in which science by itself can penetrate into the ultimate core of nature's secrets - there can be no ultimate justification for the laws of nature except on a transcendent basis. Expressed otherwise, the concept of *order* which science assumes and with it operates is not open to scientific demonstration, for order has to be assumed in any proof or disproof. Belief in order is a *sine qua non* for science, as indeed for all rational thought. Einstein's discussion of unified field theory certainly indicated that he had abandoned a positivistic notion of science, but he declined

---

[115] *Über den gegenwärtigen Stand der Feld-Theorie,* Festschrift Prof. Dr. A. Stodola, Orell Füssli Verlag, 1929, p. 126f. Cf. also C. Lanczos's discussion of this in "Rationalism in the Physical World", *Boston Studies in the Philosophy of Science,* Vol. III, 1954-6, New York, p. 185.

to press on with the question *why* with a view to clarifying understanding of the ultimate ground of rational order on which the laws of nature rest and from which they derive their unity. Instead, he went on trying to find a solution to a unified field-theory through mathematical calculations, and failed. The mathematical texture of the universe which fascinated Einstein is a very important one to which I shall return shortly.

Meanwhile let me ask, What are we to make of the role of a so-called "natural theology"? To answer that question scientifically today two points need to be considered. a) We have to take seriously the nature of "dogmatic science" developed by scientists and theologians alike in the early Christian era, and b) examine the epistemological implications of general relativity theory in our own times.

a) In rigorous science we pursue inquiry in any field in such a way that we allow the nature of the field or the nature of the object to govern how we know it, think about it, formulate knowledge of it, and how we verify that knowledge. That applies equally to natural science and to theological science, in each of which we develop a modality of the reason appropriate to the specific nature of the object. The modality of the reason appropriate to the nature of an inanimate reality is different from what we develop in knowing an animal, and different again from that in our knowing a human person. Here we switch from an impersonal to a personal modality of our reason, but with a person we are not in a position to exercise control over him or her as the object of knowing - a human being is personally other than we are, and is more profoundly objective, for example, than a rock or a cow, for a person would object to our attempts to control him or her. However, when we turn to inquire of God and seek to know him in accordance with his Nature, there is and must be a radical change in our knowing of him in accordance with his divine nature as the Lord God the Creator of our being: we cannot objectify him in the same way. Thus before God as the object of our knowing there takes place an *epistemological inversion* of our knowing relation. In knowing God in accordance with his ultimate divine nature we can know him only through his self-revelation and grace, and thus only in the mode of worship, prayer, and adoration in which we respond personally, humbly, and obediently to his divine initiative in making himself known to us as our Creator and Lord. How God can be known must be determined by the way in which he is actually known -that is, through his self-revelation. Here the modality of the human reason undergoes a radical adaptation in accordance with the compelling claims of God's transcendent nature. That is precisely what *scientific theology*, or dogmatic science, involves: knowing God strictly in accordance with his nature, κατὰ φύσιν and in accordance with his truth or reality, κατ' ἀλήθειαν. And that, in the strictest sense, is *natural* theology, theology in accordance with the *nature* of God, κατὰ φύσιν θεοῦ.

b) Today this way of knowing has been considerably reinforced through the epistemological revolution initiated with general relativity theory in its rejection of dualism, and its finding that empirical and intelligible relations inhere in one another at all levels in nature and in our knowledge of it. This has not a little relevance for traditional natural theology. Let me refer here to Einstein's own account of this in his 1921 lecture on "Geometry and Experience".[116] With relativity theory he rejected the Newtonian dualism between absolute mathematical space and time and bodies in motion, between geometry and experience, i.e. between theoretical and empirical factors in scientific knowledge. He argued that in stead of idealizing geometry by detaching it from experience, and making it an independent conceptual system which was then used as an external framework within which physical knowledge is to be gained and organized, geometry must be brought into the midst of physics where it changes and becomes a form of natural science indissolubly bound up with physics. Instead of being swallowed up by physics and disappearing, however, geometry becomes the epistemological structure in the heart of physics, although it is incomplete without physics. It is in a similar way, I believe, that natural theology is to be rejected as a *praeambula fidei*, or an independent conceptual system antecedent to actual knowledge of God, which is then used as an epistemological framework within which to interpret and formulate real or actual empirical knowledge of God, thereby subjecting it to distorting forms of thought. To set aside an *independent* natural theology in that way is demanded by rigorous scientific method, according to which we must allow all our presuppositions and every preconceived framework to be called in question by what is actually disclosed in the process of inquiry. However, instead of rejecting natural theology altogether, what we need to do is to transpose it into the material content of theology where in a changed form it serves the epistemological structure of our knowledge of God. As such, however, it cannot be used as an external parameter or independent logical structure detached from the actual subject matter of our knowledge of God. This would be in line with a faithful interpretation of St Anselm's *Fides Quaerens Intellectum*,[117] and, I believe, with a proper understanding of natural science as it arose under the impact of the Christian doctrine of the contingent rational order of the universe.[118]

Now let us turn to *mathematics* as the language of the created universe and consider whether a realist coordination of mathematics with the rational structures of nature may open up access to God. Mathematics certainly has a remarkable effectiveness helping to disclose and describe the inherent patterns of order in the created universe. In it we elaborate symbolic systems as refined instruments enabling us to extend the range of our understanding of those patterns beyond what we are capable of without them. The significance of mathematical symbolisms, however, is to be found not in the mathematical equations themselves but in their bearing beyond themselves. Mathematics is

---

[116] *Geometrie und Erfahrung*, Preussische Akademie der Wissenschaften, Sitzungsberichte, 1921, pt. 1, pp..123-130.

[117] Consult Karl Barth, *Fides quaerens intellectum. Anselm's Beweis der Existenz Gottes*, 1931 & 1958; Alexander Broadie, *The Shadow of Scotus*, 1995, p. 9ff.

[118] Refer to my discussion "The Transformation of Natural Theology", ch. 4 of *The Ground and Grammar of Theology*, 1980 & 1998, pp.75-109.

effective because it belongs to the actual contingent world, and reflects and expresses the patterned intelligibilities embodied in it, even though they cannot be captured in abstract mathematical form. In this event mathematical propositions and equations share with the universe its contingent character, and reinforce the way in which as contingent its order points beyond itself altogether.

Let it be stressed that mathematics rigorously used does not lead to a closed necessitarian or self-explanatory system of the world, which lends itself to aprioristic thinking, but to an open contingent universe. Whenever mathematics is intimately correlated with the structures of the empirical universe it operates with open-textured or incomplete symbols, for in rigorous operation it is found to have reference outside its own system which limits the validity of its formalization.

What I wish to stress here is the necessary openness of precise mathematical propositions, which Pascal showed long before when he pointed out that in defining anything in one set of terms we must tacitly assume other terms that remain undefined. Even in the strictest mathematical operations we rely upon informal thought-structures. It is impossible to operate with a set of formally complete mathematical propositions or equations - true and effective mathematical are incomplete in themselves but are open to completion beyond themselves. That truth was established in cognate ways by Georg Cantor and Kurt Gödel. Thus, as Gödel demonstrated, in any arithmetical system of sufficient richness there are, and must be, certain propositions that are not capable of proof or disproof within the given system. That is to say, while formal mathematical systems are inconsistent and incomplete in themselves, they are open to completion and are true and consistent only by reference beyond themselves. Here we have also to take into account the fact established by Alan Turing, the Cambridge mathematician, who demonstrated through an idealized computing machine that there are mathematical functions and intelligible relations in nature that are inherently non-computable, which reinforces the open reference of the contingent nature of the universe and its rational order beyond itself altogether. Thus, as John Barrow has argued, "If the universe is mathematical in some deep sense, then the mysterious undecidabilities demonstrated by Gödel and Turing are part of the fabric of the universe rather than merely products of our minds. They show that even a mathematical universe is more than axioms, more than computation, more than logic - more than mathematicians can know."[119]

I believe that rigorous scientific and mathematical accounts of the universe of space and time have the effect of reinforcing the conception of the universe as an open system of contingent rational order that points beyond itself to a transcendent ground of rationality and order in the Creator. This does not mean that science by itself or on its own independent ground gives us access to God, but that it serves the access to God which he has given us through his Word and Light incarnate in Jesus Christ. It has a very important role in opening up the

---

[119] John Barrow, "The Mathematical Universe", *Natural Science*, May, 1989, p. 311.

scientific understanding of the space-time world to God in ways congenial to Christian faith. Thus rigorous scientific understanding of the world in accordance with its actual nature and reality, κατὰ φύσιν and κατ' ἀλήθειαν, harnessed together with the access to God given in Christian theology, has today a very significant epistemic role in opening the minds of people to faith and trust in God as Lord and Savior.

Chapter 6

John Philoponos of Alexandria: Sixth Century Christian Physicist

John of Alexandria known as Philoponos, known also as the Grammarian (γραμματικός or Professor), was a thinker of epoch-making importance in the sixth century who taught philosophy and astronomy in the great Academy at Alexandria in succession to Ammonius the son of Hermias. Like him he composed a treatise on the *Astrolabe,* a complicated astronomical instrument, the oldest to survive from the ancient world.[120] He was a powerful scientific thinker of remarkable insight who in an unusual way combined empirical and theoretic ways of inquiry evident not least his critical examination of prevailing Ptolemaic cosmology and Aristotelian physics. Throughout his life he set himself to carry through a comprehensive examination and massive attack upon the foundations of Greek philosophy, science and religion, from a distinctively Christian position, and made an epoch-making contribution to the foundations of natural and empirical science. Philoponos brought into sharp focus the profound difference between the Judaeo-Christian monotheistic belief in the creation of the universe by God out of nothing and the Aristotelian and Neoplatonic belief in the eternity of the world, and between the Christian view of the universe as endowed by God with a unitary created order of its own, and the prevailing view of classical antiquity which posited a radical separation between the temporal or earthly realm and the celestial realm which it regarded as having an invariable structure. Here there was not only a sharp confrontation of monotheism with polytheism, but a conflict between the specifically Christian doctrine that through his Word (*logos*), who became incarnate in Jesus Christ, God freely created the universe and continues freely to sustain it in matter and form out of nothing, and the Greek view that the world has been made out of preexistent matter and impregnated with divine or eternal forms of rationality. By seeking to translate into physics the teaching of St. Athanasius and St. Cyril of Alexandria and of St Basil of Caesarea, John Philoponos developed a powerful critique of Aristotelian physics and cosmology, thereby injecting into the stream of European thought fundamental scientific ideas that were later to bear fruit in the rise of modern

---

[120] See the edition by A.P. Segonds, *Traité de L'Astrolabe*, in which he reproduces the Greek text with a French translation, Paris 1981.

classical science and in the post-Einsteinian appreciation of the universe as contingent in its existence and rational order.

Unfortunately, owing to the fact that Philoponos was aligned (falsely) with the so-called `monophysite' or `non-Chalcedonian' school of theology, which was declared in the seventh century to be heretical, his revolutionary scientific ideas were not given the attention they deserved. Much of his writing was lost, although traces of his influence can be found in Arab and Western Medieval thought (e.g. Robert Grosseteste) right up to the Renaissance when interest in his writings was revived - even Galileo was to acknowledge his debt to John Philoponos. However, in our own day, due to the work of Samuel Sambursky of the Weitzman Institute of Science in Jerusalem, Walter Böhm of Vienna, and more recently of Richard Sorabji of King's College, London, attention is once more being focused on John Philoponos as one who in astonishing ways anticipated some of the most significant changes that have been taking place in our understanding of the universe of space and time. The fact that the revolution in physics introduced by Philoponos was closely connected with his controlling theological ideas, suggests to us that the great Patristic theology of Alexandria from the fourth to the sixth century may well be the most relevant theology for our modern scientific world. Philoponos was a figure of towering importance, who produced in the sixth century a revolutionary view of the physical universe that was in many ways specifically Christian, and astonishingly modern in basic scientific theory.

At the end of the last century and the beginning of this century some of the main works of Philoponos bearing on science and philosophy were given publication in Germany in the original Greek text. These were Fragments of a work of Philoponos contained in Simplicius' Commentary on Aristotle's *De Caelo* by I.L. Heiberg in 1894; further fragments in Simplicius' Commentary on Aristotle's *Physics* by H. Vitelli in 1898; Philoponos' Commentary on *Categoria*, by A.Busse in 1898; his Commentary on Aristotle's *Analytica Posteriora*, by M. Wallies in 1905, and on Aristotle's *Analytica Posteriora*, by M. Wallies in 1909; Philoponos' *Commentary on Aristotle's Meteorologica*, Book One, by M. Hayduck in 1901; his Commentary on Aristotle's *De generatione et corruptione*, by H. Vitelli in 1897; his Commentary on Aristotle's *De Anima*, by M. Hayduck in 1897; and John Philoponos' Commentary on Aristotle's *Physica*, by H. Vitelli in 1887 and 1888. Again John Philoponos' very important work *De Aeternitate Mundi contra Proclum* was made available by H. Rabe in 1899 and reprinted in 1963; and Philoponos' *De Opificio Mundi* was made available by G. Reichardt in 1897. Only some of Philoponos' theological writings have survived but, apart from a few fragments in Greek, mainly in Syriac. These were edited and published by A. Sanda in 1930. Only the following are available in translation, a collection of annotated extracts in German by Walter Böhm, *Johannes Philoponos, Grammatikos von Alexandrien*, 1967; while several citations from his Commentary on Aristotle's Physics are translated in Morris R. Cohen and I.E. Drabkin, *A Source Book in Greek Science*, fifth printing 1975.

At last, however, largely due to the energetic activity of Richard Sorabji, translations into English of some of his most important works bearing on philosophy and science are being published by the Duckworth Press, London. But what about John Philoponos' theological works which are just as important as his works on physics and cosmology, for they reveal the Christian thinking which led Philoponos to transform the very foundations of science? German translations of fragments are found in the work of W. Böhm mentioned above, which are concerned mostly with Christology and Triadology, pp.411-437. What we need is a volume publishing in English all the fragments that survive in Greek and Syriac, notably the *Diaitetes, Apology for the Diaitetes, Themata against Chalcedon, De Trinitate, Against Andrew the Arian, On the Resurrection, and a Letter to Justinian*. Meantime a very significant work has been published by John Emory McKenna, *The Arbiter of John Philoponos*, Eugene, Oregon, 1997. It should be pointed out that most works on the theology of Philoponos published hitherto are slanted against him on the ground that he is alleged to be a `monophysite' heretic, but, as we now know, there is a great deal of misunderstanding here in modern as in ancient times about what John Philoponos actually meant as he applied Christian theology to natural science, and a science-oriented terminology to interpret, defend and develop the theology particularly of St Cyril of Alexandria, who was by no means a `monophysite'.[121]

Today, we need to rethink the bearing of Christian theology on the very foundations of our culture, as it has been changing so profoundly under the impact of modern scientific discoveries, and develop a way of giving undiluted expression to the central verities of the Christian faith within the context of our scientific world in such a way that they can be properly grasped and be allowed to take root in it. What better help can we get than from studying how this was carried out in the early centuries of the Christian Church when it laid down the classical basis for Christian Theology in the great Councils of the Church and when through the brilliant work of John Philoponos they began to work out its implications for a scientific understanding of the universe of space and time as it had come from the creative power of God? I believe that to study the thought of John Philoponos along with that of Athanasius, Cyril of Alexandria and Severus of Antioch will be an immense boon for the rebuilding of a distinctively Christian outlook upon the world today.

Since the theological and scientific thinking of John Philoponos took shape within the scientific tradition of Alexandria,[122] we must give some attention to the conception of scientific method offered by Clement in the famous Catechetical School there. Particularly important for him was the inner

---

[121] See my essays: "John Philoponos of Alexandria - Theologian and Physicist", *Festschrift in Honour of Archbishop Panteleimon Rodopoulos of Saloniki*, Vienna, 1998; and "Science and Access to God: Epistemological Perspective", Pontificio Ateneo Della Santa Croce, Rome, 1998.

[122] See Richard Sorabji, *Philoponos and the rejection of Aristotelian science*, 1987, especially chapter nine on "Infinity and Creation", p. 164. See also "John Philoponos and the Scientific Culture of Alexandria", Chapter 3 of the *The Life-Setting of The Arbiter* by *John Philoponos*, pp. 93-120.

connection between faith (πίστις) and scientific knowledge (ἐπιστήμη), and the appropriate method of inquiry (ἡ μέθοδος τῆς εὑρέσεως).[123] Really to know and understand something involves a way of thinking strictly in accordance with what it actually is, that is, in accordance with its nature (κατὰ φύσιν) as it becomes disclosed in the course of inquiry, and thus in accordance with what it really is, or in accordance with its reality (κατ' ἀλήθειαν), and allow its nature (φύσις) or reality (ἀλήθεια) to determine for us how we are to think and speak appropriately of it. This called for rigorous attention to the proper development and even coining of scientific terms and their use in line with disclosure of the nature of the realities to which they were employed to refer. In this context the terms φύσις and ἀλήθεια, nature and reality, were more or less synonymous in their use. This way of scientific thinking had early been developed in Alexandria by the so-called φυσικοί, the `physical' or `natural' scientists, who insisted on asking positive questions designed to disclose the real nature of the realities into which they inquired - but because of their concern with positive questions and answers, they were nicknamed, e.g. by skeptical philosophers like Sextus Empiricus, δογματικοί, `dogmatics'. Thus there arose especially in Alexandria the conception and pursuit of δογματικὴ ἐπιστήμη or "dogmatic science", that is, rigorous scientific inquiry conducted strictly κατὰ φύσιν, in accordance with the nature or reality (κατ' ἀλήθειαν) of things. This realist `kataphysic' approach was applied to every field of inquiry, including theology, for it is the nature of the object as it becomes disclosed in inquiry that determines how authentic knowledge of it is to be gained, demonstrated and expressed. That is how careful theological exposition concerned with the nature and activity of God revealed in his Son in Jesus Christ, the incarnate reality who is both God and man in one Person, came to be regarded by the great Alexandrian theologians, like Cyril, as ἐπιστήμη δογματική. Here theological and scientific traditions flowed together, and theology and science interacted with one another epistemologically and linguistically. Owing to the fact that immense attention was devoted to the doctrines of incarnation and creation, a radical transformation in the foundations of knowledge and in cosmological outlook took place: theology and science began to be pursued together within the same unitary world of space and time so that careful attention had to be given to the whole created order as it came from God and is sustained by his Λόγος or Word. That is the context in which the theological and scientific thinking of John Philoponos, together with the interaction of his scientific and theological modes of thought and speech, is to be appreciated.

Before we proceed further it needs to be stressed that too often the thought of John Philoponos has been seriously warped by scholars when interpreted within the Latin Aristotelian tradition that became dominant in the West. Thus even the great Patrologist, Berthold Altaner, wrote of him as seeking to reconcile the teaching of the Church with Aristotelianism, which was very far from the

[123] See my account of this in *Divine Meaning. Studies in Patristic Hermeneutics*, Edinburgh, 1995, pp. 130ff & 180ff.

case, as his many critical commentaries on the works of Aristotle (preserved in part by Simplicius) make clear.[124] In face of that, it must be emphasized that we cannot understand the language of the Greek Fathers, far less their thought, by reading back Latin Aristotelianism into it, as evidently happened with the influential Boethius. For example, we cannot understand *physis* by reading *natura* into it, any more than we can understand *hypostasis* by reading it as *substantia,* or *ousia* as the equivalent of *essentia*, which tends to replace concrete Greek terms, especially as governed by dynamic divine revelation, with more abstract Latin terms. This is to take no account of what went on in Alexandria in the early centuries, when the Fathers of the Church hammered out their basic forms of thought and speech, not only in the literary culture of their day, but in the midst of the most advanced scientific achievements of the ancient world, to which John Philoponos himself contributed in a quite unparalleled way.

It was the profound interconnection between his theology and his science that was distinctive of John Philoponos. His thought moved from a base in Christian theology into physics, dynamics, optics, meteorology and cosmology, and then back again to theology, in such a way that his theological thinking and his scientific thinking affected, fertilized, and deepened one another, in startling heuristic anticipation of modern scientific advances. His science cannot be adequately understood in abstraction from his theology, while his theology may not to be appreciated except in the epistemological depth and precision it gained from his conflict with traditional Hellenistic philosophy and science. John Philoponos' theology cradled in Alexandria was grounded in the incarnational, Christological and Trinitarian teaching of Athanasius and Cyril, but also in that of Severus of Antioch, all of whom rejected the epistemological and cosmological dualism of the Platonic and Aristotelian tradition. In the course of his critical and creative engagement with that tradition, Philoponos himself developed distinctive forms of thought and speech that were at once scientific, unitary and dynamic in their slant. Of central significance was the way in which he brought the Hebraeo-Christian doctrine of the mighty living God and the creation of the universe of space and time out of nothing to bear in sharp criticism upon Neoplatonic and Aristotelian notions of the eternity of the world. As already noted, much of his work in theology has not survived, some of it only in Syriac translations, but we may give attention here particularly to the *De aeternitate mundi contra Proclum, De aeternitate mundi contra Aristotelem*, together with his biblical account of the creation of the world in *De opificio mundi*. It is in the light of the transformation of thought and deep change in the meaning of technical scientific and theological terms that resulted from all this, that Philoponos' specifically theological works such as the *Arbiter* or Διατητής are properly to be understood. However, it was when the latter was read by the Byzantines through the twin spectacles of Plato and Aristotle that they failed to

---

[124] See *Ioannis Philoponi in Aristotelis Physicorum libros commentaria*, edit. by H. Vitelli, Berlin, 1887.

appreciate his theology, as well as his science, accused him of both monophysite and tritheist heresy, and pronounced misguided anathemas against him!

Already Christian theologians like Athanasius, Basil, and Cyril had begun to think out the Christian understanding of God and the world in ways which John Philoponos realized had far-reaching implications for classical philosophy and science. Three basic points may be noted. (a) The biblical doctrine of the one God, the Creator of all things visible and invisible, called in question Greek polytheism and pluralism, polymorphism and dualism, and called for a unitary view of the created universe which required a scientific way of knowing that answered to its rational order. (b) The Biblical view of the goodness of the creation, reinforced by the doctrine of the incarnation of the eternal Logos or Son of God within the creation, destroyed the idea that sensible and empirical events are not open to rational thought, and established instead the reality of the empirical world in the recognition that the temporal and sensible realities have a common rationality of a contingent kind (ἐνδεχόμενος) open to scientific investigation and understanding. (c) The fact that God himself, in creating the universe out of nothing, has conferred upon it one comprehensive rational order, had the effect of destroying the Aristotelian and Ptolemaic separation between the sensible and intelligible worlds, and so between terrestrial and celestial mechanics, and at the same time gave rise to dynamic and relational concepts of space and time as the bearers of rational order in the created universe.[125] That was the Christian view of God and the created universe which John Philoponos inherited and set out to defend against Neoplatonic and Aristotelian attacks, and on that basis to deepen and develop scientific and theological understanding of the created order.

I would like to direct attention particularly to the bearing of John Philoponos' theology on his science at two major points: (1) the impact of the doctrine of *creatio ex nihilo* upon the Greek conception of the universe; and (2) the import of the theological distinction between uncreated light and created light upon science. Both of these are found in his critical examination of Neoplatonic and Aristotelian philosophy and science, and in his constructive work on the creation of the world.

(1) *The import of the doctrine of the doctrine of creatio ex nihilo upon the Greek conception of the universe.*

It was in Alexandria, the great centre where classical science and cosmology had reached its height, but in which a stultifying amalgam of Neoplatonic and Aristotelian metaphysical ideas had come to prevail under the teaching of Proclus, that John Philoponos launched his attack upon the pagan idea of the eternity of the world, *De aeternitate mundi contra Proclum*, and followed it up by *De aeternitate mundi contra Aristotelem*, with a series of critical commentaries on the works of Aristotle. In these two works alone he set out a

---

[125]   Cf. my book *Space, Time and Incarnation*, Oxford, 1969, and Edinburgh, 1997.

philosophico-scientific account of the Christian doctrine of *creatio ex nihilo* (ἐκ μὴ ὄντος), and of the unitary universe with a rejection of epistemological and cosmological dualism that obstructed scientific investigation of empirical and cosmological realities. In them, with clever use of Aristotle's arguments against himself, he demolished Aristotle's notion of the *aither* or so-called "fifth element"[126] and with it the myth of eternal cycles and unending time,[127] and he advanced a powerful account of the real non-necessary nature of the universe created by God out of nothing but endowed with a contingent rational order of its own, which called for heuristic and experimental modes of inquiry, i.e. for *empirical science*. Of particular importance for Philoponos was the idea that God created both matter and form out of nothing[128], that is, out of non-being into being (ἐκ τοῦ μὴ ὄντος εἰς τὸ ὄν)[129], out of nothing at all, or what does not by any means exist (ἐκ τοῦ μηδαμῇ μηδαμῶς ὄντος),[130] but created it in a non-temporal way, while creating time itself along with the world.[131] These were not new conceptions for Christians but they were now expounded by Philoponos not simply as articles of faith but in a rigorous scientific and a scientific theological way, with wide-reaching implications for understanding of the whole created order. Characteristic of his scientific inquiries, pointed out by Böhm, were the experiences and experiments he described in reaching scientific theories[132]; while Sambursky referred to the brilliance of his ideas sparkling with originality and ingenuity and acute and independent criticism, and a striking scientific imagination.[133]

After many years engaged in scientific and epistemological arguments with Neoplatonists and Aristotelians, John Philoponos turned to offer something more specific about the Christian doctrine of creation by way of an interpretation of "the cosmogony of Moses", known in the history of thought as *De opificio*

---

[126] Cf. Aristotle, *De coelo*, 1; and Philoponos, *Contra Proclum* (edit. by Hugo Rabe, 1899), XIII, 485-491.

[127] Cf. Aristotle's *Physics*, 8.1; Philoponos, *In physica*, *Fragment* 108 & *Contra Proclum* (Edit. by Hugo Rabe, 1963), I.6-8, p. 17f, XI.12.

[128] *Contra Proclum*, IX.11-13; *Contra Aristotelem, Fragmenta in Physica*, 115-116, 189, 191 (cited by W.Böhm, *Johannes Philoponos*, 1967, p.309f.

[129] *De Aeternitate Mundi Contra Proclum*, XI.12 (edit. by Hugo Rabe, 1963), p. 458.

[130] See *De Aeternitate mundi Contra Aristotelem, in Physica*, 189; cf. also fragment 73, *in de Caelo*, 136-138, cited by C. Wildberg, op.cit. p. 87.

[131] See the *Fragment* 108-126 & 132, from Philoponos's commentary on Aristotle's Physics, cited by Christian Wildberg, *Philoponos Against Aristotle on the Eternity of the World*, 1987, pp. 122ff, 128ff.

[132] Walter Böhm, *Johannes Philoponos...Ausgewählte Schriften,* , p.12; cf. also p. 31. Böhm has called *Gedankenversuche* and *Gedankenexperimenten*, pp. 12, 108f, 120f, 144ff, 154f etc.

[133] S. Sambursky, *The Physical World of Late Antiquity*, p. 156.

mundi. This is what he wrote in his preface. "My long discourse concerning the creation of the world has extended to many treatises, unfolding the various reasonings and impassable labyrinths, through which those of august philosophical reputation believed to have shown that the world has not come into being, thereby running the risk of believing that God is not at all its Creator, nor has produced it out of non being. Indeed I have shown that it has a beginning of being, reasoning this out in many ways. On this account many have continuously troubled us and have in a somewhat gentle fashion reproached us, alleging that I have labored for the refutation of external reasonings beyond my power and somehow have neglected the God-given statement of the great Moses concerning the production of the world, although those who take pride in having thought out the arrangement of the universe deride these statements, as if Moses did not speak of the nature of things according to the phenomena. Especially your good self, Oh Sergius [Patriarch of Antioch], my most honoured head, who is the greatest ornament among those who serve as God's high-priests, have prompted me greatly and even forced me to contribute to the subject according to my own power. Cooperator with you in this proposed study was the well known Athanasius who is no less a man as regards piety, and who ran along with you like a young puppy beside him who brought it up in virtue. A bright mind makes youth through exercise in words."

Then speaking of the purpose of his treatise on the creation of the world, *De Opificio mundi*, and Moses' intention in his writing about the creation of the world, Philoponos added: "Many and by no means simple studies on this treatise have been attempted by many authors and especially by the well known Basil, who was adorned with every wisdom, divine and human. Since, however, some of its parts are still being questioned, because they are believed not to be in agreement with the phenomena, although Basil rightly omitted them, when he announced his own discourses on the church, for he regarded them unfitting for the untrained ear and mind, I shall try with God's cooperation to investigate these as much as it is in my power."[134]

It was thus with reference to St Basil's, *Homilies on the Hexaemeron*, an exposition of the first chapter of the book of Genesis, that John Philoponos brought his scientific understanding to the biblical account of creation.[135] It was this distinctly Christian view of the world that had opened up for Philoponos a genuinely scientific approach to an understanding of the world, freed from the philosophical myths of the Greeks. In his work Basil had rejected arguments for the eternity and necessary existence of the world, including the fabrication of a "fifth element".[136] Philoponos argued that the world was freely created by God

---

[134] I am much indebted to the Very Rev Dr George Dragas of Hellenic College, Brookline, for this translation, and also for helping me through several of his papers to understand John Philoponos' Greek text.

[135] Refer to my discussion of St Basil's thought work in *The Christian Frame of Mind, Reason, Order, and Openness in Theology and Natural Science*, 1989, pp.16.

[136] *Hexaemeron*, I.11.

and did not have to exist, for it has both a beginning and an end, and rejected as atheistic the idea that the universe came into being either by chance or fate. God created the universe out of nothing instantly (ἀκαριαίως) and timelessly (ἀχρόνως).[137] The origin of the universe, its beginning (ἀρχή) in time, and time itself, are to be traced back to a transcendent or absolute beginning (ἀρχή) in the beneficent nature and sovereign freewill of God (τῇ βουλήσει τοῦ θεοῦ)[138], the *Pantocrator*.[139] A transcendent beginning is difficult for us to conceive or express, for we can only apprehend things beyond or above time in a temporal way. Time came to exist along with the creation of the universe out of nothing. As such the universe did not have to be. By its very nature, therefore, it is intrinsically contingent and incomplete (ἀκατασκεύαστος)[140] - far from being self-sufficient or self-explanatory, its creation out of nothing in being and form is to be understood from its temporal beginning to its end only in terms of its contingence upon God and his creative Will and Word. Like Athanasius the Great Basil laid immense weight upon the fact that the universe was created out of nothing by the Λόγος or Word of God, and that it has been endowed with a orderly arrangement (διακόσμησις) that derives from and reflects a transcendent ground in the wisdom of God.[141] He took seriously the Genesis account of creation through the majestic fiat of God, including the creation of light: "Let there be light, and there was light." And distinguished this created light from the uncreated spiritual Light of the divine Logos.[142] The creative command of God brought into being the orderly sequences and enduring structures in the world of time and space - the Voice of God in creation gave rise to the laws of nature (νόμοι τῆς φύσεως).[143] Expressed the other way round, this means that all the laws of nature, all its intelligible order, are to be regarded as dependent on the Word of God as their ultimate source and ground. Hence even physical law must be treated as a contingent form of order which is finally intelligible only as it points beyond itself to the transcendent ground of intelligibility in the Logos of God the Creator and Sustainer of the universe.[144]

---

[137]   *Hexaemeron*, I. 6.

[138]   *Hexaemeron*, I.6.

[139]   Basil. *Hexaemeron*, I.1-3.

[140]   *Hexaemeron*,I.11.

[141]   *Hexaemeron*, I.8-10 & II.2.

[142]   *Hexaemeron*, VI.2 - at the same time he distinguishes the `immaterial light' (τὸ αὕλον φῶς) of the second day in the Genesis account from the stars which are the vehicles of light.

[143]   Basil, *Hexaemeron*, III.1ff; IV.1ff; V.1ff; IX,3.

[144]   See my account of this in *The Christian Frame of Mind, Reason, Order, and Openness in Theology and Natural Science*, new edition, 1989, pp. 1 ff.

It is that Basilian and biblical doctrine of creation which is the background to John Philoponos' *De opificio mundi*, but he pointed out that one must not demand from what Moses wrote technical theories about nature (τὰς περὶ φύσεως τεχνολογίας).[145] That was a point he took up again with reference to the φύσικοι - we have no way of knowing how God created things[146]. Philoponos' aim was rather to lead human beings to the knowledge of God. He took up the distinction drawn by Basil between a beginning and an absolute beginning, in recognition that a real beginning is distinct from what begins from it, and that God's creation of the world out of nothing carries with it the creation of time as well.[147] Philoponos interpreted that in a Christological perspective, and right away identified the divine wisdom through which the creation took place with the Son (1 Cor.1.24; John 1.5; Col. 1.16, 20). He is the creative Word of all things (ὁ τῶν ὅλων δημιουργὸς λόγος).[148]

It is noteworthy that John Philoponos like Basil evidently did not take the word "day" to refer a definite period of twenty-four hours, but to an unspecified period - as in the biblical statement that for God "a thousand years are as a day".[149] Basil had already pointed to the fact that the Greek text at Genesis 1.3, did not speak of "first day", but of "one day", so as not to circumscribe the duration - for what was important was its relation to eternity.[150] The divine acts of creation like that of light, "Let there be light and there was light", took place in a twinkling (ἀκαρὲς), in barely a moment, and are not to be thought of in temporal terms.[151] Of particular significance here, however, is the fact that Philoponos took up the distinction made by Basil between created light and uncreated or creative light[152], for this played a major role in his science, not only in optics, but in dynamics.

Not a little of the *De opificio mundi* was devoted to discussion and rejection of the ideas of Hipparchos and Ptolemy, but also of the teaching of Theodore of Mopsuestia, and Theodoret, and other unnamed thinkers, which need not concern us here - of much more interest to Philoponos was Basil's views of light, which I have just mentioned. This was a matter of supreme importance for science as

---

[145] See also *De opificio Mundi*, III.10. Cf. Henry Chadwick, p.51 of *Philoponos and the rejection of Aristotelian science*, by Richard Sorabji, 1987.

[146] *De Opificio mundi*, II.13: Ὅτι οὐκ εὔλογον διαπορεῖν, τίς ἡ αἰτία τοῦτα οὕτω ποιῆσαι τὸν θεὸν καὶ ἀντιπαράθεσις πρὸς Μωυσέα τῶν μετ' αὐτὸν φυσικῶν.

[147] *De Opificio mundi* (revised by Gualterus Reichardt, 1907), I.3.

[148] *De opificio mundi*, 231.1f.

[149] See Walter Böhm, op.cit. p. 408.

[150] Basil, *Hexaemeron*, II.8.

[151] *De opificio mundi*, II.18.

[152] See *De opificio mundi*, 76f.

well as theology, and for the interrelation between theology and science. It is to this we must now turn.

(2) *The import of the distinction between uncreated light and created light upon science.*

The understanding of God as Light, in a real not symbolic sense, was a basic element in the teaching of Athanasius about God as Creator and Logos: God *is* Light.[153] Due largely to the teaching of St John light had early become a primary element in Christian thought in worship and theology alike, particularly as identified with Christ.[154] Like St Basil in his *Homilies on the Hexaemeron*, John Philoponos gave attention to the Biblical account in the Book of Genesis of creation through the majestic fiat of God, including the creation of light: "Let there be light, and there was light." And he distinguished this created light from the uncreated light of the divine Logos.[155] Along with the Christian doctrine of the creation of the universe in matter and form out of nothing, and the distinction it carried between the creative activity of God and the contingent nature of the world of time and space, this was a distinction, similar to that between creative Spirit and created spirit, which became all-important for Philoponos.[156] It exercised a major role not only in his theology but in his science, and not just in optics, but in dynamics. It had the effect of reinforcing his rejection of the radical dualism in Hellenic philosophy and science between empirical and intelligible realms, between visible and invisible, tangible and intangible realities, and thus between terrestrial and celestial mechanics. It prompted him to work out in a proper scientific way intelligible relations between visible and invisible, tangible and intangible realities, and thus between terrestrial and celestial mechanics. All this called in particular for fresh thinking about the physics of light which he undertook in controversial examination of the teaching of Aristotle, especially as expressed in the *De anima*,[157] which opened the door, as we shall see, for something like a dynamic field theory (ἕξις τις) of light,[158] in astonishing anticipation of modern science.

---

[153] See, for example, *De decretis*,27, & *Ad Serapionem*,1.19.

[154] See for example the great hymn Φῶς ἱλαρόν attributed to Gregory the Theologian of Nazianzus.

[155] Basil, *Hexaemeron*, VI.2. This was a distinction also found in the West as with St Augustine, *Con. Faustum Manichaeum*, 20.7.

[156] *De Opificio mundi*, edit. by W. Reichardt, 1897, Or. II & III, and cf. p. 10, 74f, & 76ff. See also John McKenna, op.cit. Ch. 3, pp. 93ff.

[157] See Samuel Sambursky, *The Physical World of late Antiquity*, 1962, pp. 110ff; Walter Böhm, *Johannes Philoponos*, 1978, pp. 139ff, 182ff & 188ff; and Richard Sorabji, *Philoponos and the rejection of Aristotelian Science*, 1987, pp. 26ff.

[158] See Philoponos, *In De anima*, 438 b & 430 a. Cf. Böhm, op. cit. pp.176f, 188ff, 195 & 308.

In the *De anima* Aristotle had spoken of "light as the actualized state (ἐνέργεια) of some something *qua* transparent (φῶς δέ ἐστιν ἡ τούτου ἐνέργεια τοῦ διαφανοῦς ἡ διαφανές)".[159] But this was a static view of light which Philoponos rejected, and so he put forward instead a dynamic conception of light as ἐνέργεια, thereby, as Sorabji points out, changing the meaning of Aristotle's word ἐνέργεια in the process.[160] For Philoponos, ἐνέργεια imported, not change from potentiality to actuality, but real activity and movement or locomotion, but one which may be construed in relational, not mechanical, ways. Thus he spoke of light as immaterial or incorporeal dynamic force (κινητική τις δύναμις ἀσώματος, ἐνέργειά τις ἀςωματος κινητική) invisible in a medium like the air, which moves directionally and continuously at what Böhm speaks of as a timeless or practically infinite velocity ("mit praktisch unendlich grosser Geschwindigkeit").[161] This account of the movement and speed of light is also found in Philoponos' work against Proclus, where he speaks of it as so fast that it is timeless (ταχεῖα...ἡ ἄχρονος).[162]

This concept of light as incorporeal kinetic activity or as what Philoponos could call φωστικὴ δύναμις,[163] had far-reaching revolutionary implications for optics, physics and dynamics: it involved a *radically new kinetic theory*, in sharp antithesis to that of Aristotle and his concepts of the fifth element and eternal circular motion of the finite world, αἰθήρ and ἀντιπερίστασις, and the ultimate inertial motion of the unmoved mover, τὸ ἀκίνητον κινοῦν.[164]

What Philoponos did, taking his cue from the kinetic propagation of light, was to propose a new *theory of impetus* (κινητικήν τινα δύναμιν ἀσώματον), on the analogy between the impetus imparted to a projectile in being hurled and the incorporeal kinetic force (ἐνέργειά τις ἀσώματος κινητική) (or momentum) in the movement of light imparted to it by the Creator. "It is necessary to assume that some incorporeal motive force is imparted by the projector to the projectile, and that the air set in motion contributes either nothing at all or else very little to this motion of the projectile."[165] Philoponos' light theory and impetus theory amount to a radical rejection of Aristotelian physics and mechanics and register

---

[159] Aristotle, *De anima*, II.7.

[160] R. Sorabji, *Philoponos and the rejection of Aristotelian Science*, p. 26f. CF. also S. Sambursky, op.cit. p. 110f.

[161] W. Böhm, op.cit. p. 185, 187f, 315f, & 445; see also Samuel Sambursky, *The Physical World of late Antiquity*, p. 115.

[162] *De aeternitate mundi contra Proclum*, I.8.22.

[163] *In De anima*, 330.38.

[164] See W.D. Ross' selections from Aristotle's *Physics*, 1927, pp. 99-104: 28b, 28-252a4; 258b10-259a20.

[165] Translation by Cohen and Drabkin from Aristotle's *Physics* 642.9, *A Source Book in Greek Science*, 1948, p .223.

an immense advance in scientific understanding of the universe. This was congenial, as Philoponos realized, to the Christian doctrine of creation out of nothing, for God himself is the creative source of all matter and form, all light and energy in the universe.[166] Light and impetus theories together scientifically reinforced and contributed to the unitary view of heaven and earth, matter and form, space and time, freely created by God Almighty out of nothing, for it was through his eternal Word or *Logos*, the Light of the world, that he has freely endowed them with their motive force (κινητικὴ δύναμις) and continues to maintain and hold them together in their rational order.

The combination Philoponos' dynamic and relational theories of light and motion gave rise to a conception of the universe governed throughout by an internal cohesion (ἕξις) affecting and unifying all activity within it.[167] *Thus light theory and impetus theory constituted together a kind of dynamic field theory.*[168] The immediate effect of this was to liberate science from the closed mechanical world of Aristotle, nowhere more apparent than in his quantitative conception of space as the immobile limit within which a body is contained,[169] and replace it with a unified open-structured world by a contingent non-necessary kind of rational order. The change in the conception of space applies, *mutatis mutandis*, also to John Philoponos' relational conception of time in the reciprocal bearing of time and motion upon one another. All this had the effect of profoundly altering the fundamental conception of the nature (φύσις) of things, and consequently of the understanding of scientific inquiry as pursued strictly "in accordance with the nature (κατὰ φύσιν) of things", that is, in accordance with what things really or actually are (κατ' ἀλήθειαν), and therefore in accordance with their dynamic nature or natural force (κατὰ τὴν φυσικὴν δύναμιν). This change to a radically dynamic and relational conception of the inherent order and nature of the universe carried with it a radical change in the pursuit of objective scientific inquiry itself and correspondingly in the precise meaning and handling of scientific terms. That was nowhere more evident than in the dynamic use and meaning of "nature" or φύσις itself, and of "reality" or ἀλήθεια, e.g. in their frequent synonymous relation with one another.[170] It cannot be emphasized too strongly that it is in this light that both the scientific and the theological writings

---

[166] *In De anima*, 330, 21 & 418 b 9.

[167] For the use of ἕξις in this way see Philoponos *In De Anima*, 418b & 430 a; and cf. W. Böhm, op.cit., pp. 195 & 308.

[168] Thus also John McKenna, op.cit. p. 100f.

[169] See my account of this in *Divine Meaning. Studies in Patristic Hermeneutics*, 1995, pp. 296ff. Platonic, Aristotelian notions of space had, of course, already been rejected in Nicene Theology - see my discussions in *Space, Time and Incarnation*, 1969, pp. 1-21, and *Divine Meaning*, pp. 343-373.

[170] See J. Lebon, *Corpus Scriptorum Orientalium*, pp. 180f, cited by Iain R. Torrance, op. cit, p.15; and Lebon, *Le Monophysism Severien*, 1909, p.304, cited by John McKenna, op.cit. p. 88 f.

of John Philoponos are properly to be understood. Samuel Sambursky once wrote: "The terms `natural' and `according to nature' and `contrary to nature' make sense only with regard to a system of reference, and if that system is a partial one, the correct terminology might be the reverse of that for a system which is regarded as a whole."[171] It was in failing to take this into account that interpreters of John Philoponos, ancient and modern, have often erred badly, i.e. in trying to understand him by dragging his thought back into the Aristotelian frame of reference from which he sought to emancipate science and theology alike.

We must not overlook the fact that already in the development of Alexandrian theology, particularly through Athanasius and Cyril, there had come about a steady development in the use of theological terms. Thus in their actual use φύσις, οὐσία, ὑπόστασις, πρόσωπον, had already been stretched, changed, and developed under the dynamic impact of the Gospel, so that attention must be given to their actual use in particular contexts rather than to their classical definitions. Thus in the doctrines of Christ or the Holy Trinity they become strictly *theological terms*, and are not to be used (except in a secular context) in their classical Platonic, Aristotelian or Stoic sense. The problem that arose was nowhere more sharply evident than in respect of the Cyrilian concepts of μία φύσις τοῦ θεοῦ λόγου σεσαρκωμένη, and ἕνωσις καθ' ὑπόστασιν φυσικήν. Particularly important was the fact that the terms φύσις and φυσική, which had acquired a dynamic and scientific slant especially through the work of Athanasius and Cyril,[172] but also of Severus of Antioch[173] to whom John Philoponos was particularly indebted. With them the term φύσις could be used in several related and pleonastic ways, with a proper variation in accordance with the demands of reality. Thus on the one hand Athanasius used it differentially of uncreated and created being, but on the other hand he could also use it as more or less the equivalent or a synonym of reality, ἀλήθεια or οὐσία, as in the expression κατὰ φύσιν where to think in accordance with the nature of something is to think truly, ἀληθῶς, of it. Moreover, as we have already noticed, the term φύσις in Alexandria had also come to be used in a scientific sense to denote "reality", as in rigorous scientific inquiry where to know something strictly "in accordance with its nature", κατὰ φύσιν, is to know it "in accordance with its reality", κατ' ἀλήθειαν. It was after all in this sense that Athanasius had

---

[171] Samuel Sambursky, *The Physical World of Late Antiquity*, 1962, p. 96f.

[172] Cf. my discussion of these basic patristic/theological terms in *Theology in Reconciliation*, 1975, pp. 239ff; *Divine Meaning*, 1995, pp. 202ff; and also Methodios G. Fouyas, *The Person of Jesus Christ in the Decisions of the Ecumenical Councils*, 1976, pp. 65ff. See further, *Divine Meaning, Studies in Patristic Hermeneutics*, 1995, "The Hermeneutics of Clement of Alexandria, pp. 130ff and "The Hermeneutics of Athanasius", pp. 229-288.

[173] See Iain R. Torrance, *Christology After Chalcedon, Severus and Sergius the Monophysite*, 1988, pp. 14ff.

understood and used the term *physis* to speak of a reality that confronts us in its own independent being, and which is known in accordance with its own inherent force in virtue of which it is and continues to be what it actually is. And it was in that concrete sense of *physis* that he could speak of Christ as the incarnate Word or Son of God.[174] It was because that was not recognized or understood by the Aristotelian establishment in Byzantium that John Philoponos was condemned and then anathematized as a monophysite heretic, which had the disastrous effect of condemning and rejecting his revolution in natural science, resulting in its loss for many, many centuries. In fact it was not until the revolutionary change that started with the work of James Clerk Maxwell in the combination of light theory and impetus theory that our modern empirico-theoretical science actually arose.

In that context the Athanasian and Cyrilian expression μία φύσις σεσαρκωμένη, used by John Philoponos, referred to "one incarnate reality", indeed one undivided Being or Person (one *ousia* or *hypostasis*, and in *that* sense also as one *physis*) without any rejection of the truth that Jesus Christ is God and Man in one Person, one incarnate reality both perfectly divine and perfectly human. The *mia physis* was just as important for Philoponos, as it had been for Athanasius and Cyril for whom it affirmed the oneness of the incarnate Word of God (μία φύσις τοῦ θεοῦ λογοῦ σεσαρκωμένη). That is to say, like Athanasius and Cyril, John Philoponos would have nothing to do with a schizoid understanding of Christ for in him God and Man were one Reality and Person, but that does not mean that Philoponos was a "monophysite" in the heretical sense, any more than was Athanasius or Cyril.

The theology of John Philoponos, in particular his doctrines of Christ and of the Trinity, is properly to be understood in terms of the interrelation between his theological and scientific thinking. It was in the light of his Christian belief that the world was created out of nothing by the eternal Word of God who became incarnate in Jesus Christ that Philoponos engaged in his rigorous scientific work, in demolishing the Platonic and Aristotelian idea of the eternity of the world, and arguing for the contingent non-necessary nature of the world and its rational order. In so doing Philoponos, as we have seen, developed a remarkably *dynamic* understanding of science, with a corresponding change in his understanding, use and meaning of scientific terms. This reflected back on his theology, in particular on his doctrines of creation, incarnation and redemption, which he came to understand in a more *dynamic* way, and to express in correspondingly *dynamic* modes of thought and speech. His doctrines of Christ and the Trinity were essentially the same as those of Athanasius and Cyril of Alexandria, but he brought to their expression a scientific *kataphysic* precision, in line with his anti-Aristotelian science, and his non-Aristotelian understanding and use of technical terms, such as those of φύσις, οὐσία, ὑπόστασις, ὕπαρξις, πρόσωπον, which had a particularly significant place in the theological controversies that followed upon disagreement over the dualist ingredient detected in the Chalcedonian

---

[174] See again my account of this cited by Archbishop Methodios in *The Person of Jesus Christ in the Decisions of the Ecumenical Councils*, Addis Ababa, 1976, p. 65.

formula.[175] Thus, for example, Philoponos refused to think of οὐσία in terms of Aristotle's distinction between first and second substance, and refused to use φύσις in a static way, but used it in a dynamic relational way, and indeed in a differential way where cross-level relations were involved, as in the relation between the deity and humanity of the incarnate Son of God.

When read in this light his controversial work Διαιτητής, *Arbiter*[176], must be understood in an orthodox way in line with a brief statement of his belief in the Incarnation of the Savior in agreement with holy Scripture: "The eternal Son, the only begotten Word of the Father, true God of true God, equal in Being [consubstantial] with his Begetter, at the end of the ages, truly became incarnate of the blessed Mary, Mother of God, and came forth as a perfect man, absolutely without having suffered variation or change in his own being but united himself hypostatically to a human body, animated with a rational soul."[177] Philoponos pointed out that the term φύσις does not always mean the same thing, for it can have a general and a particular use.[178] Thus φύσις can be used in a way that is strictly in accordance with the reality to which it is actually being used to refer without any contradiction, that is, if it is understood dynamically and relationally in the light of its objective reference, and not just in accordance with Aristotelian rules for logical division and classification or some formal system of logical definitions and distinctions. Philoponos could certainly use logical and dialectical argument to great effect in analyzing and demolishing the arguments of opponents, as when he turned Aristotle's idea of infinity against himself.[179] As a realist scientist and theologian, however, John Philoponos was a φυσικός and δογματικός concerned with dynamic reality, not with abstract or philosophical investigations. It is difficult to see how anyone who thinks objectively and relationally in this way can accuse Philoponos of being a monophysite in the heretical sense, for it would seriously misconstrue his essentially dynamic *kataphysic* way of thinking.

Later on in the Διαιτητής[180], he points out that the word φύσις has a general significance as when referring to the nature of a man or a horse, but it can also have a particular significance in accordance with reference to some particular reality. It is in this particular way that the Church in its doctrine speaks of the

---

[175] See *The Tome of Leo*, III & IV.

[176] See the edition by A. Sanda, 1930, and the translation and excerpts published by W. Böhm, op.cit. pp. 414.

[177] Latin edition of *Diaitetes seu Arbiter*, by A. Sanda, 1930, p. 37.

[178] See again Sanda's edition of the *Diaitetes seu Arbiter*, 57, and the translation and excerpts by Böhm, op.cit. p. 417.

[179] See Richard Sorabji, *Time, Creation and the Continuum*, 1983, pp. 210ff, and *Philoponos and the rejection of Aristotelian Science*, 1987, p. 168f.

[180] Sanda's text, 57 & 58 - see *Patrologia Graeca* 94, 748 & 752; cf. Böhm, op.cit. p. 317.

Father, the Son and the Holy Spirit who are one Nature, but also of the Nature of three distinctive Hypostases or Persons. Here the term φύσις is used appropriately of the one Nature of God the Father, the Son and the Holy Spirit, but also appropriately of the Son in accordance with his distinctive Nature. Philoponos is clearly affirming the Orthodox doctrine of the Trinity, but in his dynamic and realistic way, and not in accordance the use of φύσις as defined within a table of categories in terms of genus and species commonly found in the schools. It is evident, however, that if what Philoponos has written were interpreted in a accordance with Aristotelian logical distinctions, he could be misconstrued as putting forward a heretical notion of the Trinity - however, that would be a serious hermeneutical mistake to say the least. And of course elsewhere, for example in his *De aeternitate mundi contra Proclum*, he had put forward the traditional formula about the Trinity, *Three Persons, One God*, without any demur or equivocation.[181] How he could have been honestly accused of "tritheism" it is difficult to understand, unless it was because the terms he used were taken in their Aristotelian sense by theologians like Photius, and were thus wrongly construed in an abstract dialectical way. He certainly did not believe in "three Gods" as was alleged by Aristotelian theologians like Photius. He was no more a "tritheist" than a "monophysite" in the heretical sense, but a scientific theologian who insisted on using theological terms in the doctrines of Christ and the Trinity in an appropriate *dynamic* way, strictly κατὰ φύσιν or in accordance with the particular realities indicated and in accordance with the Gospel. Thus it is refreshing to read the assessment of Walther Böhm: "Ingesamt muss man sagen, dass die monophysitische Christologie in dieser geläuterten und gemässigten Form, wie sie Philoponos und ebenso schon vor ihm Severus, auf den er sich stützt, präsentiert, kaum noch als häretisch bezeichnet werden kann. Sie steht in ihren positiven Aussagen, wenn man die Begriffe so nimmt, wir sie gemeint sind, mit der dogmatisierten Lehre der katholischen and orthodoxen Kirche nicht in Widerspruch."[182]

Here is the text of his *Credo* which John Philoponos incorporated in a letter to the Emperor Justinian.[183]

"The Son of God and the Word, the Makers of all things, who is from everlasting God with God the Father, who begat him who is above the ages and through whom God even the Father has made the ages, the same who in these latter days has become a man, when he was incarnate by the Holy Spirit and by the Theotokos, the ever-virgin Mary, whose flesh is consubstantial with us, and possesses a rational and reasonable soul, while his divinity is not changed into flesh, and whose holy flesh is not changed into divinity, the same who was

---

[181] *De Aeternitate Mundi Contra Proclum*, VI 4 & 5, pp. 237 & 239.

[182] W. Böhm, op.cit., p. 413.

[183] Translated by John McKenna, op.cit. p. 135.

*crucified in flesh, our Lord Jesus Christ, who willingly tasted death on
our behalf and after three days rose from the dead and ascended into
heaven, who is one of the blessed and consubstantial Trinity.*

My concern now is not to pursue that further but to discuss the fruitful way
in which through John Philoponos, theologian and physicist, Christian theology
and natural science can bear fruitfully upon one another. John Philoponos did not
intrude his theology upon his science, or his science upon his theology. However,
his theological grasp of divine truth opened his eyes to a more realistic
understanding of the contingent nature of the world and its distinctive rational
order, and exercised a regulative role in his choice and formation of scientific
concepts and theories and their explanatory development. At the same time the
dynamic character of his physical science, as it arose in this way, had a bearing
upon the dynamic character of his theology, and deepened his grasp of its
epistemological ground and perspective.

He never thought of arguing from the world to the Creator, for that would
have presupposed a logically necessary relation between them, No, he regarded
the world as created freely by God and endowed with a contingent form of
rationality different from God's transcendent Rationality, but as such pointing
openly beyond itself to the Creator. That is to say, his Christian theology opened
up for him access to science, and his science thus understood opened up for him
access to God. It was the theological distinction between the uncreated Light of
God and the created light of the world that was all-important for him. It impelled
him to develop the physics of light in a dynamic open-structured way, which
radically changed the foundations of ancient science. In so doing John
Philoponos anticipated the kind of empirico-theoretical science in which we
engage today on the foundation laid down by James Clerk Maxwell when he
brought light theory and impetus theory together in his epoch-making work *A
Dynamical Theory of the Electromagnetic field.*[184] It was his concept of the
continuous dynamic field that Einstein hailed as the greatest change in the
rational structure of science.[185] What lay behind that change, however, which
Einstein did not realize, was Clerk Maxwell's adaptation to physics of the kind of
onto-relations expressed in the Christian doctrine of the Holy Trinity, in which

---

[184] Refer to my edition of this work in 1982, reprinted in 1997; and to my account of his
thought in *Transformation and Convergence in the Frame of Knowledge,* 1984, ch. 6,
pp. 215-242; in *Senso del divino e scienza moderna,* tr. by G. Del Re, 1992, pp. 317-
352; and in *Das Verhältnis zwischen christlichem Glauben und moderner
Naturwissenschaft. Die geistesgeschichtliche Bedeutung von James Clerk
Maxwell,*1982.

[185] Albert Einstein, Leopold Infeld, *The Evolution of Physics,* 1938, "Field, Relativity",
pp. 125 ff; also, Einstein, *The World as I See it,* pp. 156-161; and Einstein's
appreciation of Clerk Maxwell, pp.29-32, in my edition of *A Dynamical Theory of the
Electromagnetic Field.*

the relations between the three divine Persons belong to what they really are.[186] That way of thinking out in a non-necessary, non-mechanistic, and non-logical way, the dynamic relations of light particles with one another in the magnetic field, revealed the kind of access which Christian theology can have to natural science, and thereby also revealed the kind of access on *epistemological grounds* that natural science can have for Christian theology. It is, I believe, in this epistemological perspective, in which we engage in the conceptual interface of theological and natural science, that we may rightly ask questions about the way in which natural science, pursued in this dynamic relational way hand in hand with theology, can open for us today a mode of access to God.

In the rest of this address I want to discuss the way in which we may consider the kind of access which natural science in relation to theological science may be said to serve access to God. Theologians and scientists live and work within the same empirical world of space and time, which both theologians and scientists have to take seriously, when there is inevitably an overlap in their inquiries, and in the modalities of the reason which they develop under pressure from the different realities with they have to do. How then, in our modern era, may we think of the access of natural science to God?

Of massive significance, of course, is the concept of *contingence*, contingent reality and contingent order,[187] upon which all our modern science, particularly since Clerk Maxwell and Einstein, is based.[188] As we have already noted it was the Biblical concept of *creatio ex nihilo* by Christian theology that made empirical science rationally possible and indeed gave rise to its early beginnings. By contingence is meant that the whole universe of matter and form was freely created by God and endowed with a rationality of its own utterly distinct from the transcendent rationality of God, but dependent or contingent on it. It is a serious error to think of contingence as chance or to equate the contingent with the accidental, but that is what is often being put forward today by scientists, especially in the field of biology. Appeal to chance is a way not to think, but contingence refers to a positive form of rational order which is not self-explicable but points beyond itself to a transcendent ground of order as the ultimate reason for what it is. In the nature of the case contingence is not something that natural science could ever have come up with and cannot explain - and yet all our natural science and the laws of nature which it seeks to formulate have to do with the intrinsically contingent nature of the universe and its contingent form of rationality. This means that natural science cannot explain itself, and that there is no way of arguing from the contingent nature or rationality of the world explored by science to God, for that would presuppose

---

[186]   For that he was evidently indebted to Robert Boyd, *Praelectiones in Ephesios*, 1661, cc. 487 et seq.

[187]   I have discussed this at length in *Divine and Contingent Order*, 1981 & 1998.

[188]   Refer to my contribution to *John Paul II On Science and Religion. Reflections on the New View from Rome*, 1990, pp. 105ff.

that the world is not contingent but necessary. It cannot be said, therefore, that natural science or the world of nature which it explores and seeks to comprehend, actually gives us access to God. However, because the world is contingent in its rational order, by its very nature it points openly beyond itself, and cries out, so to speak, mutely for the Creator. Far from closing access to God natural science is an open door to a way of knowing God beyond itself. By the very nature of its contingent rational order, natural science reaches out in its formulation of the laws of nature beyond the boundary of being with non-being, in a tacit semantic reference to some form of "law beyond law", to an ultimate *why* or a *transcendent reason* for the laws which it formulates. In virtue of its contingent nature the world is not finally understandable without relation to God.

That was the issue raised by Albert Einstein in his remarkable lecture in Zürich in 1929 on the present state of field theory, when he claimed that science has now reached the point where we cannot remain satisfied with knowing *how* nature is, and *how* its laws operate, for we want to know *why* nature is what it is and not otherwise (*warum die Natur so und nicht anders ist*). He went on to say that to aim at a "logical uniformity" somehow related to God would be a "promethean" undertaking, but here nevertheless science has to do with the "religious basis" of its scientific struggle (*die religiöse Basis des wissenschaftlichen Bemühens*).[189] That is to say, there is no way in which science by itself can penetrate into the ultimate core of nature's secrets - there can be no ultimate justification for the laws of nature except on a transcendent basis. Expressed otherwise, the concept of *order* which science assumes and with it operates is not open to scientific demonstration, for order has to be assumed in any proof or disproof. Belief in order is a *sine qua non* for science, as indeed for all rational thought. Einstein's discussion of unified field theory certainly indicated that he had abandoned a positivistic notion of science, but he declined to press on with the question *why* with a view to clarifying understanding of the ultimate ground of rational order on which the laws of nature rest and from which they derive their unity. Instead, he went on trying to find a solution to a unified field-theory through mathematical calculations, and failed. The mathematical texture of the universe which fascinated Einstein is a very important one to which I shall return shortly.

Meanwhile let me ask, What are we to make of the role of a so-called "natural theology"? To answer that question scientifically today two points need to be considered. a) We have to take seriously the nature of "dogmatic science" developed by scientists and theologians alike in the early Christian era, and b) examine the epistemological implications of general relativity theory in our own times.

---

[189] *Über den gegenwärtigen Stand der Feld-Theorie,* Festschrift Prof. Dr. A. Stodola, Orell Füssli Verlag, 1929, p. 126f. Cf. also C. Lanczos's discussion of this in "Rationalism in the Physical World", *Boston Studies in the Philosophy of Science,* Vol. III, 1954-6, New York, p. 185.

a) In rigorous science we pursue inquiry in any field in such a way that we allow the nature of the field or the nature of the object to govern how we know it, think about it, formulate knowledge of it, and how we verify that knowledge. That applies equally to natural science and to theological science, in each of which we develop a modality of the reason appropriate to the specific nature of the object. The modality of the reason appropriate to the nature of an inanimate reality is different from what we develop in knowing an animal, and different again from that in our knowing a human person. Here we switch from an impersonal to a personal modality of our reason, but with a person we are not in a position to exercise control over him or her as the object of knowing - a human being is personally other than we are, and is more profoundly objective, for example, than a rock or a cow, for a person would object to our attempts to control him or her. However, when we turn to inquire of God and seek to know him in accordance with his Nature, there is and must be a radical change in our knowing of him in accordance with his divine nature as the Lord God the Creator of our being: we cannot objectify him in the same way. Thus before God as the object of our knowing there takes place an *epistemological inversion* of our knowing relation. In knowing God in accordance with his ultimate divine nature we can know him only through his self-revelation and grace, and thus only in the mode of worship, prayer, and adoration in which we respond personally, humbly, and obediently to his divine initiative in making himself known to us as our Creator and Lord. How God can be known must be determined by the way in which he is actually known -that is, through his self-revelation. Here the modality of the human reason undergoes a radical adaptation in accordance with the compelling claims of God's transcendent nature. That is precisely what *scientific theology*, or dogmatic science, involves: knowing God strictly in accordance with his nature, κατὰ φύσιν and in accordance with his truth or reality, κατ' ἀλήθειαν. And that, in the strictest sense, is *natural* theology, theology in accordance with the *nature* of God, κατὰ φύσιν θεοῦ.

b) Today this way of knowing has been considerably reinforced through the epistemological revolution initiated with general relativity theory in its rejection of dualism, and its finding that empirical and intelligible relations inhere in one another at all levels in nature and in our knowledge of it. This has not a little relevance for traditional natural theology. Let me refer here to Einstein's own account of this in his 1921 lecture on "Geometry and Experience".[190] With relativity theory he rejected the Newtonian dualism between absolute mathematical space and time and bodies in motion, between geometry and experience, i.e. between theoretical and empirical factors in scientific knowledge. He argued that in stead of idealizing geometry by detaching it from experience, and making it an independent conceptual system which was then used as an external framework within which physical knowledge is to be gained and organized, geometry must be brought into the midst of physics where it changes

---

[190] *Geometrie und Erfahrung*, Preussische Akademie der Wissenschaften, Sitzungsberichte, 1921, pt. 1, pp..123-130.

and becomes a form of natural science indissolubly bound up with physics. Instead of being swallowed up by physics and disappearing, however, geometry becomes the epistemological structure in the heart of physics, although it is incomplete without physics. It is in a similar way, I believe, that natural theology is to be rejected as a *praeambula fidei*, or an independent conceptual system antecedent to actual knowledge of God, which is then used as an epistemological framework within which to interpret and formulate real or actual empirical knowledge of God, thereby subjecting it to distorting forms of thought. To set aside an *independent* natural theology in that way is demanded by rigorous scientific method, according to which we must allow all our presuppositions and every preconceived framework to be called in question by what is actually disclosed in the process of inquiry. However, instead of rejecting natural theology altogether, what we need to do is to transpose it into the material content of theology where in a changed form it serves the epistemological structure of our knowledge of God. As such, however, it cannot be used as an external parameter or independent logical structure detached from the actual subject matter of our knowledge of God. This would be in line with a faithful interpretation of St Anselm's *Fides Quaerens Intellectum*,[191] and, I believe, with a proper understanding of natural science as it arose under the impact of the Christian doctrine of the contingent rational order of the universe.[192]

Now let us turn to *mathematics* as the language of the created universe and consider whether a realist coordination of mathematics with the rational structures of nature may open up access to God. Mathematics certainly has a remarkable effectiveness helping to disclose and describe the inherent patterns of order in the created universe. In it we elaborate symbolic systems as refined instruments enabling us to extend the range of our understanding of those patterns beyond what we are capable of without them. The significance of mathematical symbolisms, however, is to be found not in the mathematical equations themselves but in their bearing beyond themselves. Mathematics is effective because it belongs to the actual contingent world, and reflects and expresses the patterned intelligibilities embodied in it, even though they cannot be captured in abstract mathematical form. In this event mathematical propositions and equations share with the universe its contingent character, and reinforce the way in which as contingent its order points beyond itself altogether.

Let it be stressed that mathematics rigorously used does not lead to a closed necessitarian or self-explanatory system of the world, which lends itself to aprioristic thinking, but to an open contingent universe. Whenever mathematics is intimately correlated with the structures of the empirical universe it operates with open-textured or incomplete symbols, for in rigorous operation it is found to

---

[191] Consult Karl Barth, *Fides quaerens intellectum. Anselm's Beweis der Existenz Gottes*, 1931 & 1958; Alexander Broadie, *The Shadow of Scotus*, 1995, p. 9ff.

[192] Refer to my discussion "The Transformation of Natural Theology", ch. 4 of *The Ground and Grammar of Theology*, 1980 & 1998, pp.75-109.

have reference outside its own system which limits the validity of its formalization.

What I wish to stress here is the necessary openness of precise mathematical propositions, which Pascal showed long before when he pointed out that in defining anything in one set of terms we must tacitly assume other terms that remain undefined. Even in the strictest mathematical operations we rely upon informal thought-structures. It is impossible to operate with a set of formally complete mathematical propositions or equations - true and effective mathematical are incomplete in themselves but are open to completion beyond themselves. That truth was established in cognate ways by Georg Cantor and Kurt Gödel. Thus, as Gödel demonstrated, in any arithmetical system of sufficient richness there are, and must be, certain propositions that are not capable of proof or disproof within the given system. That is to say, while formal mathematical systems are inconsistent and incomplete in themselves, they are open to completion and are true and consistent only by reference beyond themselves. Here we have also to take into account the fact established by Alan Turing, the Cambridge mathematician, who demonstrated through an idealized computing machine that there are mathematical functions and intelligible relations in nature that are inherently non-computable, which reinforces the open reference of the contingent nature of the universe and its rational order beyond itself altogether. Thus, as John Barrow has argued, "If the universe is mathematical in some deep sense, then the mysterious undecidabilities demonstrated by Gödel and Turing are part of the fabric of the universe rather than merely products of our minds. They show that even a mathematical universe is more than axioms, more than computation, more than logic - more than mathematicians can know."[193]

I believe that rigorous scientific and mathematical accounts of the universe of space and time have the effect of reinforcing the conception of the universe as an open system of contingent rational order that points beyond itself to a transcendent ground of rationality and order in the Creator. This does not mean that science by itself or on its own independent ground gives us access to God, but that it serves the access to God which he has given us through his Word and Light incarnate in Jesus Christ. It has a very important role in opening up the scientific understanding of the space-time world to God in ways congenial to Christian faith. Thus rigorous scientific understanding of the world in accordance with its actual nature and reality, κατὰ φύσιν and κατ' ἀλήθειαν, harnessed together with the access to God given in Christian theology, has today a very significant epistemic role in opening the minds of people to faith and trust in God as Lord and Savior.

---

[193]   John Barrow, "The Mathematical Universe", *Natural Science*, May, 1989, p. 311.

Chapter 7

The Relevance of Christian Faith to Scientific Knowledge with Reference to John Philoponos and James Clerk Maxwell

The foundations of modern science were laid down during the first six centuries through the preaching of the Gospel and the teaching of the Holy Scriptures about the creation of the world out of nothing and the redemptive incarnation of the Word of God in space and time in Jesus Christ. This had the effect of destroying the dualist foundations of classical philosophy and science, and of revealing the contingent nature of the universe and its God-given rational order. The doctrine of the mighty living and acting God undermined the rationalistic and inertial system of Aristotelian philosophy and science, and made possible the rise of empirico-theoretical science as we know it. In actual fact during those early centuries Christian theologians and scientists made signal cognitive and empirical contributions to science which anticipated some of the epoch-making advances of the nineteenth century on which present day science rests.

In this brief contribution to the Notebook of Pascal Centre I shall limit myself to three principal ways in which Christian faith has made effective cognitive contributions to science: in respect of 1) Rigorous scientific method, 2) Direct input, 3) Regulative impact.

1) *Scientific method*. Rigorous scientific method was worked out by Christian theologians in Alexandria from the second to the fifth centuries in the face of Aristotelian, Neoplatonic, and Sceptical philosophers. Careful thinking in theology and science alike proceeds strictly in accordance with the nature or objective reality of what is being investigated and/or interpreted, that is in accordance with what it really is. This called for a process of positive questioning of realities or framing of thought experiments designed to let their actual nature to disclose itself - a method which became known as "kataphysic" or "dogmatic science", that is a science in which thinking and knowing are positively governed by the objective nature or reality of things, operate holistically rather than analytically, and develop a modality of the reason that is appropriate to the specific nature of the object whether it be a rock, tree, an animal, or a person. Thus a switch in the modality of the reason takes place when one moves from one objective reality to another - the scientific method remains the same, to know

it as strictly as possible in accordance with its nature, whether an inanimate or animate reality, a static or an active reality. But a more radical change takes place in the case of a human being, another rational agent over whom the inquirer can have no control, but where the inquirer responds to him/her and reveals something of his/her inner self. Here there takes place a two-way relation, a personal interaction, between the knower and the one known. While the modality of the reason changes accordingly, the scientific method remains the same, knowing and thinking of the other strictly and adaptively in accordance with his/her nature.

When we turn to inquire of *God* and seek to know him in accordance with his nature, the modality of our reason undergoes a very radical shift, but the scientific method remains the same: knowing him strictly and holistically in accordance with his divine reality and nature. Here human thinking undergoes an epistemic reorientation, a *metanoia*, under the creative and self-revealing impact of God's personal interaction with us. Thus there takes place an *epistemological inversion* of our knowing relation but in strict accordance with the nature of God as he makes himself known to us. With creaturely realities we seek to know them in accordance with their nature as they become `disclosed' to us under our questioning, but with God our knowing of him in accordance with his nature takes place under the constraint of his activity in `revealing' himself to us. Here scientific method, pursued strictly in accordance with the nature and reality of God as he makes himself known to us is up against a measure of objectivity that we encounter nowhere else, under the compelling claims of his transcendent nature which we can never master. This means that we may know God truly only through his self-revelation and grace, and hence only in the mode of worship, prayer, and adoration, in which we respond humbly and obediently to his divine initiative in making himself known to us personally and savingly through his Word as our Creator, Lord and Savior.

It is a form of the same scientific method that was held by Christians in the Early Church to apply to the understanding and interpretation of the Holy Scriptures which call for a deep seated change of mind, appropriate to the reality and nature of God's *Word* as it is mediated to us in and through the Scriptures. That is to say, the Holy Scriptures were to be interpreted objectively in accordance with the nature of the divine Realities and Activities to which they direct us. In them God has adapted his self-revelation to human language in such a way, that human statements in the Scriptures direct us beyond themselves to God, so that in seeking to understand and interpret the Scriptures as given us by God, the divine reality they mediate, the very Word of God himself, is not to be subordinated to the human word, but the human word to the divine reality to which they refer. Scientific method requires us, therefore, to give careful attention both to the human character of the Scriptures and to the transcendent Nature of God, but in so doing to take the Reality of God's self-revelation to us in the Scriptures so seriously that we look through the human word to the divine Reality of God's self-revealing Word mediated to us in and through the Scriptures. It was much the same relation that Christians found to obtain between the activity of natural scientists and the realities they seek to understand: when the scientist inquires into the nature of the contingent world, he does that not by looking at God but by looking away from him at the world, but when the theologian inquires into the nature of God, as he has revealed himself to us he does that not by looking at the nature of the world, which God created out of nothing, but by looking away from the world to its Creator. In both instances the scientist and the theologian seek to act strictly in accordance with the nature of the objective reality into which he inquires.

2) *Direct input.* Never in all the history of science has Christian theology had such a transforming impact on science as through *John Philoponos* of Alexandria in the sixth century. His was a biblical and Christocentric theology in which he developed the Christian conception of the creation of the universe out of nothing and sought to give an adequate account of its contingent rational order. Of particular importance for him was the Biblical teaching about the incarnation of the Creator Word of God in Jesus Christ, the Light of the world through whom all things were made, and of the intrinsic relation between the divine Word and the divine Light. Working with a distinction between uncreated Light and created light, he put forward a theory of light and a theory of impetus, which together overthrew the static inertial notions of Aristotelian science, and produced a dynamic understanding not only of sciences such as optics, physics, and meteorology, but of the unitary universe of heaven and earth. In the course of this transformation of classical science he advanced relational conceptions of time and space, defining them in terms of the dynamic of what he called "light force". This called for a new holistic way of thinking of real intelligible relations with which traditional Aristotelian and Euclidean logic, concerned with static patterns and relations, could not cope, which came under severe attack particularly from Aristotelian philosophers and scientists like Simplicius known as The Commentator. However, the overthrow of a static for a dynamic theory of light, and the transformation of physics it involved, was an astonishing anticipation of the role of light put forward by Clerk Maxwell and Einstein more than a thousand years later.

It should be added that, in accordance with Philoponos' conception of the contingent nature of the universe and its rational order, as also in accordance with his doctrine of the creation of the world out of nothing freely through the Word of God incarnate in Jesus Christ, Philoponos would have nothing to do with any attempt to argue from the nature of the world to the existence of God, for that would have meant that God is necessarily related to the world, and that would imply that the world was not freely created by him out of nothing, while nevertheless endowed with a form of rational order utterly distinct from God but dependent on him. While science, transformed under the impact of Christian theology, points properly away from itself to God, this is because of the Christian theological input into an understanding of its contingent nature.

The work of John Philoponos represents an outstanding instance of the direct cognitive *input of Christian beliefs* in the development of natural science. Of signal importance in it was the relation between the uncreated Light and Word of God, and created "light" and creaturely "word". This relation between light and word involved an informational input into scientific theory beyond what could be extracted by way of reflection upon the activity of the physical light in the cosmos by itself. Physical light was, and had to be, understood not merely through its empirical behavior, but through the bearing upon it of information which shaped its theoretical content. Expressed otherwise, it was through a "meta-relation" of light to "word", and above all to the Word of God, that it came to be understood and deployed by Philoponos in his transformation of science. It was thus through the cognitive content of his faith that Philoponos actually developed his epoch-making light theory and impetus theory. This raises for us the importance of what we call "information theory", and the need to take into account some sort of transcendent order, or "meta-plan", in developing scientific theory especially at boundaries between being and non-being. That is, of course, particularly clear today in respect of the human genome which is laden with more information than would fill a vast encyclopedia, and which by its astonishing complex nature could not have arisen in some sort of accidental or self-organisational way.

John Philoponos' development of dynamic science led to a significant *feed-back* into Christian theology, not in content but by way of developing its dynamic character in accordance with the redemptive activity of the incarnate Word of God. This had already been taking place, particularly through the thought of the great theologians, Athanasius and Cyril of Alexandria. Now, however, the interrelation between this theology and science, which had given rise to dynamic science, rebounded upon Philoponos' theology in respect of his scientific method and technical terms, giving them a more dynamic form. The crunch came when basic theological terms were given a dynamic slant in accordance with the dynamic nature of the realities to which they referred. That meant that they could not be interpreted in their classical literary sense, that is, as read in accordance with the meanings they had in classical Greek literature, and as read particularly through the twin spectacles of Plato and Aristotle. Thus crucial terms and expressions referring to the nature and oneness of the incarnate Son of God came under severe attack from the Byzantine Establishment. For example, when Philoponos cited Cyril's expression, "the one incarnate nature of the Word of God", and interpreted it holistically in accordance with his one dynamic reality and not analytically, he was accused of being a monophysite heretic - that is, one who denies that Christ was both divine and human - anathematized, and his writings banned, with the result that science, and the cognitive relation of theology to science, not least the cognitive input of theology in science, were obstructed until modern times. The rejection of Philoponos had the disastrous effect of allowing Aristotelian science, with its inertial concept of God as the Unmoved Mover and its logico-analytical modes of thought in theology and science, to overrun Western culture and to give rise to the dualist and deterministic conception of the world that stems from Galileo and Newton.

3) *Regulative impact.* In modern times there arose a new Philoponos, *James Clerk Maxwell*, a devout evangelical believer, whose light theory and impetus theory together also gave rise to a *dynamical* way of scientific thinking, which broke free from the kind of mechanistic science based on Newton's *Principia Mathematica*, and opened up the way with his dynamic field theory of light for

the transformation of science through relativity and quantum theory. The decisive change came with the publication of Clerk Maxwell's epoch-making book, *A Dynamical Theory of the Electromagnetic Field*, 1864, which according to Einstein brought about the greatest change in the axiomatic basis of physics and correspondingly in our conception of reality. This was followed by Clerk Maxwell's two-volume work *A Treatise on Electricity and Magnetism* in 1873, which must be reckoned with Newton's *Principia Mathematica* as one of the two great works on which modern science rests.

Clerk Maxwell did not intrude theological ideas specifically or directly into his scientific theories, but the Christian faith deeply entrenched in his being exercised a *regulative role* in the choice and formation of his leading scientific concepts. Thus the cast of his mind, shaped through an intuitive apprehension of the relation of God to his creation, provided him with what he called "a fiducial point or standard of reference" for discriminating scientific judgments. It directed him to real ends external to himself, and to the kind of real objectivity he needed for critical scientific activity, not least in grasping and bringing to appropriate expression the intelligible relations inherent in nature. This called for a holistic rather than an abstractive way of thinking, in which he could let real dynamic relations have their full value, without being mauled by abstract Aristotelian logic. Hence he inverted the current mathematical and scientific way of beginning with analytical particulars and building up the whole by synthesis, but made primary a mathematico-conceptual mode of interpreting dynamic realities and real ontological relations without distorting them. At the same time his Christian faith provided Clerk Maxwell with certain "analogical truths", root ideas, and fundamental conceptions, for which natural science could not account but which guided him in the scientific task of wedding thought with reality and developing appropriate ideas. He spoke of these as "modes of thought" and "physical truths" matched to the unveiling of processes inherent in nature, which called for a corresponding mode of "physical reasoning" and a "new mathesis in mathematics" particularly concerned with ontological relations of space and time relations.

Clerk Maxwell became convinced that "in a scientific point of view the *relation* is the most important thing to know". The kind of relations he wanted to express and develop were not of a putative kind but real relations of an ontological kind inhering in reality, for the inter-relations of things are ontologically constitutive of what they really are. The relations between things, even of persons, belong to what they are. That was a conviction deeply rooted in Scottish theology and metaphysics which Clerk Maxwell was to call to his aid when again and again he failed to offer a satisfactory explanation of the of the moving lines of force in the electromagnetic field in terms of Newtonian physics and mechanics. Thus when he developed an explanation of the behavior of electro-magnetic particles, in particular of the way in which light particles, relate ontologically and dynamically with one another moving at the speed of light, he came up with the concept of the *continuous dynamic field*, which had the effect of transforming the laws of classical Newtonian mechanics, and opening the way toward a new understanding of physical reality in terms of relativity and quantum theory. This was a revolutionary counterpart to the transformation of Aristotelian science by John Philoponos in the sixth century through the combination of light theory and impetus theory. It was not that Clerk Maxwell imported theological conceptions as such into his science, but rather that the pressure of his Christian understanding of God and his creation of the world led him to put forward new ideas and ways of thinking that transformed the basic structure of natural science, and were congenial to the Christian understanding of the universe of space and time. In other words, it was his basic Christian beliefs that prompted his new scientific thinking and exercised a *regulative* role in the choice and formation of his leading scientific concepts.

What, then, about the relation of *light* to *word*, created light to the uncreated Light and Word of God, the transcendent Source of all contingent order in the universe? It is to Clerk Maxwell that we owe the discovery that light has mathematical properties. Everything we know in the universe, macrocosmically or microcosmically, we learn from light signals, but their mathematical patterns have to be deciphered and coordinated with word in the formation of scientific theory and the development of knowledge. That is to say, as Philoponos taught, *information* is needed in understanding the behavior of light and its divinely given dynamic role in the universe. Created light by its very nature, points away to the uncreated Light and Word of God, the ultimate ground of all rational order and the transcendent source of the information needed in the development of science. Philoponos and Clerk Maxwell together thus point us in seeking understanding of the universe toward some meta-source of knowledge or meta-order to guide our research and develop appropriate scientific theory. It is, I believe, along these lines that we may profitably think out for our generation the cognitive bearing of Christian belief upon the advance of scientific knowledge of the universe that God has made and within which his Word became incarnate in space and time.

Chapter 8

Michael Polanyi and the Christian Faith: *A Personal Report*

Michael Polanyi was born of Jewish parents in Hungary, but before or after his engagement to Magda Polanyi, a Christian, he committed himself to the Christian Faith and in 1919 was baptized in the Roman Catholic Church. When I came to know Michael and Magda Polanyi, I realized that like her he was a Christian believer, but claimed that he did not have a strong feeling or urge toward Roman Catholicism, for in Hungary he felt that Catholicism was tarnished by an unfair treatment of the Jews. His thinking reveals the impact of classical Christian thought, such as that of St Paul and St. Augustine. He felt rather differently about Protestant Christianity, but was shocked by what he found in Germany. On the completion of his University studies in Physical Chemistry and Medical science, he became a medical officer in the Austro-Hungarian Army, when he reflected not a little about the relation between medical and scientific thinking and faith and activity. In his first academic appointment to a chair in Berlin, he lived near Albert Einstein, who at that time was married to a Serbian Orthodox scientist whom he had met in his studies in Switzerland, and who had an impact on his religious beliefs. However, she declined to live with him in Berlin, due to her antipathy to Germans, and they were divorced. I know of nothing bearing directly on Christian belief in her relations with Einstein. But in Berlin Einstein came under severe attacks from militant Nazis - again and again they prevented Einstein, from getting the Nobel prize when he was in Berlin, and finally obstructed the awarding of the Nobel prize to him for his work on relativity theory. When the Nobel Prize was finally given to Einstein it was for his work on Brownian motion, not for relativity theory. The situation became so hostile in Germany that Einstein wisely left Berlin for Princeton, to join the newly established Institute for Advanced Studies and Research, and there became known for his sympathy to Protestant Christian thought. He hung on the wall of his study a Portrait of James Clerk Maxwell, the most devout and evangelically committed Christian scientist who, he claimed, had fundamentally altered the rational structure of science. There, probably due to him, the main avenue on the campus was called "Maxwell Avenue". In Princeton Einstein was also befriended by Christian clergy and theologians in Princeton Theological Seminary, and lived on its campus, with theologians on both sides of his house.

Although Michael Polanyi was committed, as he once wrote, to the transcendent origin of his beliefs - "unless you believe, you will not understand", he reiterated. There is no evidence (known to me) of any discussion between Polanyi and Einstein about Christian belief. But in Princeton Einstein was daily in contact with Christian believers, theologians and scientists, and without doubt Christian institutions in the University and the City. One of Polanyi's school friends in Budapest, John von Neumann, was also given at post at the Advanced Institute. Eugene Wigner, one of his first pupils in Germany and a very good friend had been given a chair in physics in Princeton University, but when he tried to get Polanyi to join him there, he was obstructed by fiercely anti-Marxist Americans who confused Michael with his brother. In Manchester it was Professor T. W. Manson, the Principal and Vice-Chancellor of the University, a noted New Testament scholar, and a Scots Presbyterian, who befriended Michael Polanyi and used to take him to worship in the Presbyterian Church which Manson attended. As a Christian believer Michael Polanyi took God as real and worship as important, and often referred to the latter, as also to the Pauline conception of salvation by grace, as analogous to the process of scientific discovery. Gracious and modest with high moral standards, his theology was largely "tacit" in his distinctive sense of that term and deep-seated. Both Polanyi and Manson were rather critical of the Marxist, and anti-Christian thinkers, such as Professor Blackett, and their positivist philosophy of natural and social science, in Manchester. Michael Polanyi engaged in critical discussion with Blackett and other Marxists in the University and their positivist notions of science and philosophy. He does not seem to have had a close contact with Bernard Lovell, the Radio Astronomer at Jodrell Bank, although he and Magda played tennis with him and his wife Joyce, a cousin of my wife Margaret.

Michael regarded the relation between faith and reason as fundamental, and was committed to restore the priority of belief even in science: he loved to recall the Augustinian statement, "Unless you believe, you will not understand" (actually it derives from Clement of Alexandria!). In face of the growing impact of secularism being fostered by Marxist naturalism on society, he felt increasingly the need to restore believing commitment to academic and scientific pursuits. It was clear to Polanyi that the relation of faith and reason in the Christian tradition, and classical ways of thinking about science and society, needed to be recovered. Man needs a purpose in science as in life that bears on eternity, as he wrote at the conclusion of his little book *The Tacit Dimension*. "Perhaps this problem cannot be attained on secular grounds alone. But its religious solution should become more feasible once religious faith is released from the pressure by an absurd vision of the universe, and so there will open up interest a meaningful world which could resound to religion." Although that was written in 1966, it was these convictions that led him to ask for a new chair in the Philosophy of Science to be established, in his desire to counter the programme of secularist science and materialist and positivist scientific method in British Universities which was distorting the understanding of science through a false and deadening scientism, and to foster free personal inquiry sustained by commitment and heuristic vision which was fostered by Christian worship. It was under this conviction that his early books *Faith, Science and Society*, and *The Logic of Liberty*, were published. A new Chair concerned with post-critical thinking, heuristic knowledge and the philosophy of science was established in spite of sharp opposition and Michael Polanyi was appointed to it. Through that chair he was concerned to restore the balance between faith and reason in science, and to argue for the concept and pursuit of pure science dedicated to the service of a transcendent reality, free from all temporal authority.

Bernard Lovell was somewhat disappointed not with Polanyi's convictions but with the idea he was moving from his chair in pure Chemistry made famous by Dalton. However it became more and more clear that it was the role of religious commitment, and indeed of belief or the kind of faith found in the Christian tradition, evident in his frequent appeal to St Paul and St Augustine, that came to occupy an underlying role in his Polanyi's post-critical basic heuristic thinking both in science and philosophy. That was later given outstanding exposition in his Aberdeen Gifford Lectures which he entitled *Personal Knowledge*. His conception of reality even in science, and of the all-important role of meaning in science, had undoubtedly a deep Christian orientation and feeling, even if it did not betray an explicitly asserted or denominational commitment. Yet it is as impossible to be religious, Polanyi used to say, without having a religion, as it is impossible to speak without having a language. Christian inquiry, he insisted, is worship, and it is as such that it fosters the kind of heuristic vision and inquiry that break free from traditional frameworks of thought into what is quite new. He once wrote: "Christian worship sustains, as it were an eternal, never to be consummated hunch, a heuristic vision which is accepted for the sake of its irresolvable tension. It is like an obsession with a problem known to be insolvable, which yet follows, against reason, unswervingly, the heuristic command: `Look at the unknown!'. Christianity sedulously fosters, and in a sense permanently satisfies, man's craving for mental dissatisfaction by offering him the comfort of a crucified God."[194]

"The assumption that the world has some meaning, which is linked to our calling, as the only morally responsible beings in the universe, is an example of the supernatural aspect of experience which Christian interpretations of the universe explore and develop".[195] Polanyi often referred to the creative power in the universe which meets our striving in terms of the Christian word for "grace". That is very evident, for example, in the way in which the personal character and thrust of his scientific thinking and activity were due to a deep Christian commitment influenced particularly by St Paul's teaching about redemption and Augustine's stress upon faith as the door to understanding, and upon the objective nature of meaningful reality. That was a primary aspect of Michael's thinking which, it seems to me, was set aside by Harry Prosch in his editing and reworking of Polanyi's book entitled "Meaning" in which he reverted to what

---

[194] Cited by Drusilla Scott from *Personal Knowledge*, p.199, *Everyman Revived, The Common Sense of Michael Polanyi*, 1985, p,185.

[195] Drusilla Scott, op.cit. p.,186.

Drusilla Scott (recalling *The Tacit Dimension*, p. 32f) called "a cobblestone definition of reality" ![196] That appeared to be a merely symbolical and phenomenalist conception of reality and free floating meaning which Michael Polanyi, in his conversations with me in Oxford, rather resented and repudiated. That is why, as I shall relate, he asked me to act as his literary executor after his death so that kind of twisting of his thought and his writings could not take place. What we miss in *Meaning*, as Prosch edited it, is the bearing in Michael Polanyi's thought of the actual effect of divine action in the life of people, and its objective ground and force. Thus, for example, the resurrection, would have no meaning for Christians if it had not actually taken place. Thus, as Drusilla Scott says: "What we miss in *Meaning* and what Polanyi's whole thought leads us to, is this actuality; the effect in the lives of ordinary suffering men of what actually happened in the life and death of Jesus, and of the meaning for them that these events revealed."[197]

I myself did not get to know Michael Polanyi until after he had delivered his Gifford Lectures in Aberdeen entitled, *Personal Knowledge. Towards a Post-Critical Philosophy*, published in 1958. He had been proposed as Gifford Lecturer by my friend Professor Donald MacKinnon who then held the Chair of Moral Philosophy in Aberdeen University and was enthusiastically supported by Principal Tom Taylor. Donald had got to know Michael Polanyi in connection with the *Moot* (probably in 1944), a high-level group of Christian thinkers assembled by J.H. Oldham during the war who met in the Athenaeum in London. He had invited Michael Polanyi to join them in discussing important *Christian issues* pressing upon the Church and society as a result of the war. I was not a member of the Moot - John Baillie had objected to my being a member as a "Barthian" ! Nevertheless I was asked by Oldham to present them with a paper in reaction to one by the philosopher H. A. Hodges of Oxford, who had a special interest in the writings of the German Philosopher, Wilhelm Dilthey. That was in August 1941. I was very familiar with the work of Dilthey, whom I cited fully in my reply to Hodges, but was not present at that meeting of the Moot in The Athenaeum in London, nor was Michael for he did not actually become a member until later. I was greatly excited by the Aberdeen Gifford Lectures when published in 1958. And so I arranged with John Baillie to have Michael Polanyi invited to give us some lectures in New College, Edinburgh, when our friendship began. Before long I was to get to know him very well in Oxford. Polanyi had by then retired from Manchester to a house in Oxford. There he was invited to become a Fellow at Merton College, where for several years until his death he took part in the life and worship of the College, where one of my friends, John R. Lucas, a devout Anglican, was the resident Philosopher who was deeply concerned with mathematics and physics, and space and time. But that was the hey-day of the linguistic philosophy dominated by the positivist and logicist thinking of the Vienna Circle, and its Oxford counterpart the linguistic

---

[196]   Op. cit, p. 190.

[197]   Op.cit, p. 194.

philosophy and logical positivism of Gilbert Ryle and A.J. Ayer, the very kind of arid meaningless philosophy, hostile to Christian theology, of which Polanyi was very critical!

That was the situation in Oxford in 1969 when my book *Theological Science* was published by the Oxford University Press in which I had given not little attention to Michael Polanyi's thought, and was critical of Ryle and Ayer. Michael welcomed it very warmly, and we became fast friends, and met not infrequently when I was back in Oxford. After he read my *Theological Science* and we engaged in discussion about the relation of science to faith and theology, his Christian commitment seemed to be more and more firm and open (or less tacit!). I also got to know his dear wife Magda rather well, and was welcomed by her and Michael as a clergyman, as well as a theologian, in their home at 22 Upland Park Road, and stayed with them as a frequent visitor - that in fact became my home from home in Oxford. When I stayed with Michael and Magda there or nearby, I learned how devout both he and she were and sensed the deep quiet Christian spiritual affinity between them. As a rule Michael Polanyi was rather reticent about discussing his own religious beliefs, for some of his ardent supporters in the philosophy of science, like Marjorie Grene, were, I learned, rather hostile to religion. However, from my personal relations with them in their home, I had no doubt about the quiet depth and commitment of his faith, and of Magda's Christian devotion as well. As I learned from Magda, Marjorie Grene was rather hostile to her, as she did her best to shelter Michael from the attentions of admiring women!

In the rather critical thought of Oxford in those days, the Polanyis were not befriended very much by College Dons, nor by the Anglican clergy but were by the Methodist minister who lived near them, and they not infrequently attended his Church. One of their best friends was Lady Drusilla Scott, the wife of a retired Diplomat, and the daughter of the Scottish Philosopher, A. D. Lindsay the former Master of Balliol. Michael and I had common friends, T. M. Manson and Donald Mackinnon. We were also associated through our membership of the International Academy of the Philosophy of Sciences, a Dominican foundation based in Brussels. Some of Michael's most important papers were given there, and printed in the Proceedings of the Academy, as well as elsewhere, and were later edited by Marjorie Grene and published by Routledge & Kegan Paul in 1969, as *Knowing and Being*, the year when the Oxford University Press published my *Theological Science*. Einstein was a member of the Academy, but I never saw him there. Karl Popper was also a member, but he and Michael did not get on very well together for, as Magda told me, Michael felt that Popper had "pinched" some of Michael's distinctive ideas on the nature of scientific discovery, such as those presented in his paper, "The Unaccountable Element in Science", later published in *Knowing and Being*. Evidently when Polanyi was present at the Academy, Popper stayed away, and when Popper was present Polanyi often was not! Another member of the Academy was Freddie Ayer, but it was a Dominican foundation, and I noticed him only once at a special anniversary meeting in Brussels after Polanyi had died.

Michael told me that he found my book *Theological Science* rather difficult because of its theological content, but appreciated what I had tried to do in it - in arguing for a proper realist scientific approach to theology - and applauded it! *Theological Science* was a revision of lectures I had given in the USA in 1959. When in our discussion about it I asked Michael about his occasional references to Paul Tillich, he told me that he had turned away from his thought; and when I asked him about the relation of his thinking to French philosophers like Merleau-Ponty, he insisted that he was not a phenomenalist. It was then that he told me about his chagrin and disappointment with what Harry Prosch had done in his editing and presentation of *Meaning* which had been published by Chicago University Press under both their names. In editing it Prosch had given a somewhat phenomenalist slant to Michael Polanyi's post-critical thought as a movement away from his critique of scientific objectivity, with a rather mystical view of Christianity, detached from the actual historical events and objectivity of the Christian message. In speaking of what Prosch had done, Michael referred to the fact that after the death of Einstein, something similar had been done in the presentation of his writings when they had sometimes been twisted round in an alien way. That was, Michael felt, rather like what Harry Prosch had done to his thought in *Meaning*. Then he turned to me, and asked me if I would act as his literary executor after he died, to prevent that sort of thing happening again. And I promised to do so. That is also why I have never referred to the book *Meaning* in what I have written about Michael Polanyi and his thought, for it distorts it rather seriously especially after chapter three. However, someone called Colin Weightman has now published a book called *Theology in a Polanyian Universe. The Theology of Thomas Torrance,* in which he accuses me of misunderstanding Polanyi, but has in fact, I believe, severely misunderstood Polanyi and my theology. In it he has in fact bowdlerized my interpretation and use of Polanyi's thought, charged me with not paying attention to *Meaning*, and backed up his attack on me by references to *Meaning*!!

Unlike Prosch Michael Polanyi, as I knew him, was certainly a Christian. Of particular importance in assessing his devout Christian commitment and belief, which he never paraded, is the powerful chapter in *Personal Knowledge* which he entitled "The Critique of Doubt". In it he wrote of the Christian faith as "a passionate heuristic impulse". "A Christian impulse can live only in the pursuit of its proper enquiry. The Christian enquiry is worship. The words of prayer and confession, the actions of the ritual, the lesson, the sermon, the church itself, are the clues of the worshipper's striving towards God. They guide his feelings of contrition and gratitude and the craving for the divine presence, while keeping him safe from distracting thoughts...Only a Christian who stands in the service of his faith can understand Christian theology and only he can enter into the religious meaning of the Bible. Theology and the Bible together form the context of worship and must be understood in their bearing on it..."[198] That was how some of in Britain presented and discussed his thought in the book *Belief in*

---

[198]   *Personal Knowledge*, pp. 280 & 281.

Science and in the Christian Life. The Relevance of Michael Polanyi's Thought for Christian Faith and Life, Edinburgh, 1980.

My last discussions with Michael Polanyi, had to do, if I remember correctly, with the nature of light in the thought of Einstein and James Clerk Maxwell. I had become increasing interested in the science and faith of James Clerk Maxwell, and wanted to discuss it with him. But I had really left it too late. The last letter I had from him was after the death of his elder son George, the economist, which he and Magda felt very deeply. In it he wrote about the visit he and Magda had paid to Guildford Cathedral to celebrate Easter, where in their worship he was overwhelmed with the actual resurrection of Christ. He was not to live very long afterwards.

Magda and her younger son, John, asked me to take the funeral service in Oxford. He was a Novel Laureate Professor of Chemistry in Toronto, who had married the daughter of an Anglican clergyman in Shanghai, and attended St Thomas Church in Toronto. Alas, I was quite unable to take the funeral as I was completely tied up with my Moderatorial engagements in the Church of Scotland at that time, but my younger son, Iain, who was a postgraduate student at Oriel College, Oxford, represented me at the funeral services.

I visited Magda at 22 Upland Park Road, as soon as I could afterwards, and arranged to return to help her with Michael's papers and affairs when she confirmed that she and John wanted me to act as Michael's literary executor. This called for a long visit to Oxford to check over and make a preliminary inventory of his books and pamphlets. After some discussion she agreed to accept the offer of the University of Chicago to establish a special section of the Regenstein Library devoted to Michael's books and papers. It was hoped at first that they might be kept and housed in Oxford, but Magda needed the financial resources the University of Chicago offered for the books in support for her retirement. After a while I returned to Oxford with a friend and helper in New College, Dr Christopher Kaiser (now Professor of Theology at Western Theological Seminary in Michigan) who was both a scientist and a theologian, to assist me in making an inventory of Polanyi's papers and books, which took us several days to do. Among them I found a copy of Kurt Gödel's epoch-making little book, *Über formal unentscheidbare Sätze der Principia Mathematica und verwandter Systeme I,* which he had arranged to be made for him by Edinburgh University Library, and which he used in writing *Personal Knowledge.* It was in Edinburgh later that Gödel's work was translated by one of our mathematicians, Bruce Meltzer, and published by Oliver & Boyd in 1962. I asked Magda if I might keep that xeroxed copy in memory of Michael, to which she gladly agreed. All the other books, pamphlets, scientific papers, and relevant correspondence, from Michael's library, were duly collected by Chicago University for housing and display in their Regenstein Library. In it they lodged their own scientifically checked and prepared catalogue. They include, it may be added, the correspondence between Michael Polanyi and Thomas Kuhn, in which Kuhn admitted that he had taken the concept of paradigm from Michael!

I visited Magda Polanyi in Oxford as often as I could, and we corresponded with one another regularly for several years, until she too died to rejoin Michael in heaven waiting for the resurrection which they had already experienced together in spirit in Guildford Cathedral.

When Magda died I asked John Polanyi in Toronto to take over from me the role of literary executor of his father's works, especially as the copyright had now devolved from Magda to him. Again and again questions of copyright raised by authors in different countries, who wished to cite from Michael's writings, had cropped up, when I always consulted with Magda. But when she died I persuaded John to take over the role of literary executor from me, which he has done. I hope and pray that those who now write for *Tradition and Discovery* will remain faithful to Michael and his thought and not try to twist his ideas for their own ends.

Chapter 9

Fides et Ratio and the Theology of Science: The Relevance of Christian Faith to Scientific Knowledge

In his Encyclical Letter *Fides et Ratio* John Paul II has presented Christian believers with a remarkable statement about the relationship between Faith and Reason in which he has taken his cue from the Holy Scriptures of the Old and New Testaments about the relation between divine revelation and God's Wisdom. In it he has spelled out an account of faith and reason in which he speaks of them as the two wings on which the human spirit rises to the contemplation of truth. Under the twin rubrics of *Credo ut Intelligam* and *Intelligo ut Credam*, he has set forth in line with the historic teaching of the Roman Catholic Church and its traditional philosophy a remarkably lucid account of the relation between faith and philosophy in "the conviction that there is a profound and indissoluble unity between the knowledge of the reason and the knowledge of faith." In it he calls theology to undertake "the delicate and demanding task" which he speaks of as "the understanding of revealed truth or the articulation of the *intellectus fidei*. The *intellectus fidei* demands the contribution of a philosophy of being which first of all would enable *dogmatic theology* to perform its functions appropriately." By and large, however, throughout the Encyclical, while recalling here and there that theological truth is ultimately grounded in Christ John Paul II does not say very much offer about the positive ontological relation between faith and its proper object, the Word and Truth of God incarnate in Jesus Christ in space and time, nor does he, on the other hand, offer an account of philosophy in a determinative relation to its objective realities in the contingent structures of space and time. Hence it is understandable that in this Encyclical the Pope has offered only hints of the way in which faith and reason are ontologically related to natural science, or virtually nothing like "a theology of the sciences".

In developing or even exploring a theology of the sciences today we must be concerned not just with some tangential or historical relationship between religious beliefs and scientific enterprise, nor just in a general or abstract way with the interrelations between faith and science and science and faith, but with something rather more definite, their positive and actual bearing upon one another in method and as far as possible even in content. That is surely demanded of us as Christians who believe that the whole universe of space and time explored by natural science was created by God out of nothing and endowed with its rational order by the mighty Word of God who became incarnate in Jesus Christ within space and time. That is to say, we must give attention to the *cognitive effect* of positive belief upon the formation and development of scientific understanding and explanation, and indeed upon the rise and formation of concepts and theories in the natural sciences and mathematics. That is an objective not envisaged in *Fides et Ratio*, but which fidelity to the Gospel of the Incarnation, Resurrection and Ascension of the Lord Jesus Christ to which indeed *Fides et Ratio* rightly directs us, will not allow us pass over lightly or set aside.

There are fundamental issues at stake here, which my own concern as a Christian theologian will not allow me to evade: the deep-level *conceptual interface* between theological and scientific understanding of the rationality embedded in the created order of things. Here we have to take into consideration something of which few scientists and fewer theologians seem really to be aware, the epistemological revolution brought about through general relativity theory, the inseparability of ontological and empirical factors found in nature and in our authentic understanding of it at every level. Failure to discern and grasp this is often evident in the epistemological naiveté that characterizes even some of our most distinguished scientists, not to speak of theologians. The inherence of theoretical and ontological factors in one another applies particularly to the basic concept of order with which we have to do in all natural and theological science under a categorical imperative and obligation that is thrust upon us from an ultimate ground of order. This means that we are forced to think out natural and moral laws in terms of their intrinsic ontological grounds, and think out physical laws in terms of their contingent relations to a stable ground of intelligibility beyond themselves - the ultimate Why (to which Einstein referred in connection with unified field theory), the reason or justification of all law in God. This implies, as Clerk Maxwell and Albert Einstein, realized in their different ways, that there is and must be a fundamental harmony between the laws of the mind and the laws of nature, that is an inherent harmony between how we think and how nature behaves independently of our minds.

Thus the more profoundly our understanding penetrates into the rationality of the universe of space and time, the more clearly and fully a preestablished harmony between mind and nature becomes manifest, between the way we think and what we think about. All this applies to the interrelations of theological science and natural science, although they are both concerned in their different ways with a kind of intelligible order immanent in the created universe - that is with the *contingent* rational order with which all empirical and theoretical science have to do and upon which they are grounded.

As we now know the foundations of modern science were laid down during the first six centuries through the preaching of the Gospel and the teaching of the Holy Scriptures about the creation of the world out of nothing and the redemptive incarnation of the Word of God in space and time in Jesus Christ. This had the effect of destroying the dualist foundations of classical philosophy and science, and of revealing the contingent nature of the universe and its God-given rational order. The doctrine of the mighty living and acting God undermined the rationalistic and inertial system of Aristotelian philosophy and science, and made possible the rise of empirico-theoretical science as we know it. In actual fact during those early centuries Christian theologians and scientists made signal cognitive and empirical contributions to science which anticipated some of the epoch-making advances of the nineteenth century on which present day science rests.

In recent years I have been deeply concerned with the thought of the sixth century theologian, philosopher and scientist in the great Academy of Alexandria (not mentioned in *Fides et Ratio!*). As we now know John Philoponos did more than anyone else to transform the foundations of ancient philosophy and science, and helped to lay the foundations upon which, we now know, all our empirical and theoretical science ultimately rest. Unfortunately the works of John Philoponos were by recalcitrant Aristotelian Churchmen in Byzantium, so that what he achieved in working out a profound relation between Christian theology and natural science, was largely lost for more than a thousand years - although elements of his thinking about light and motion filtered through to the west, which we discern particularly in the thought of Grosseteste and Galileo. Thankfully the anathema against Philoponos has now been lifted, so that access to his thinking need no longer hindered in the Catholic Church. From what we now know of his thought in the sixth century, it is clear that John Philoponos anticipated the way in which James Clark Maxwell in the t century brought his Christian convictions to bear upon his mathematics and physics in such a way that, as Einstein declared, "it transformed the logical structure of science". As a result we are now able to discern much more clearly and helpfully the ways in which Christian theology and natural science, and thus also between faith and reason, bear cognitively and creatively upon one another, that we may grasp something of the profound cognitive impact of the Christian Gospel (not just of "faith") upon the scientific enterprise, and thus begin to form in our minds something of what Dr Lila Archideo has called "the Theology of Sciences".

In this brief article I shall limit myself to three principal ways in which Christian theology has made effective cognitive contributions to science: in respect of 1) Rigorous scientific method, 2) Direct input, 3) Regulative impact.

1) *Scientific method.* Rigorous scientific method was worked out by Christian theologians in Alexandria from the second to the fifth centuries in the face of Aristotelian, Neoplatonic, and Skeptical philosophers. Careful thinking in theology and science alike proceeds strictly *in accordance with the nature or objective reality of what is being investigated and/or interpreted, that is in accordance with what it really is.* This called for a process of positive questioning of realities or framing of thought experiments designed to let their actual nature disclose itself - a method which became known as "kataphysic" or "dogmatic science", that is a science in which thinking and knowing are positively governed by the objective nature or reality of things, operate holistically rather than analytically, and develop a modality of the reason that is appropriate to the specific nature of the object whether it be a rock, tree, an animal, or a person. Thus a switch in the modality of the reason takes place when

one moves from one objective reality to another - the scientific method remains the same, to know it as strictly as possible in accordance with its nature, whether an inanimate or animate reality, a static or an active reality. But a more radical change takes place in the case of a human being, another rational agent over whom the inquirer can have no control, but where the inquirer responds to him/her and reveals something of his/her inner self. Here there takes place a two-way relation, a personal interaction, between the knower and the one known. While the modality of the reason changes accordingly, the scientific method remains the same, knowing and thinking of the other strictly and adaptively in accordance with his/her nature.

When we turn to inquire of *God* and seek to know him in accordance with his nature, the modality of our reason undergoes a very radical shift, but the scientific method remains the same: knowing him strictly and holistically in accordance with his divine reality and nature. Here human thinking undergoes an epistemic reorientation, a *metanoia*, under the creative and self-revealing impact of God's personal interaction with us. Thus there takes place an *epistemological inversion* of our knowing relation but in strict accordance with the nature of God as he makes himself known to us. With creaturely realities we seek to know them in accordance with their nature as they become 'disclosed' to us under our questioning, but with God our knowing of him in accordance with his nature takes place under the constraint of his activity in 'revealing' himself to us. Here scientific method, pursued strictly in accordance with the nature and reality of God as he makes himself known to us is up against a measure of objectivity that we encounter nowhere else, under the compelling claims of his transcendent nature which we can never master. This means that we may know God truly only through his self-revelation and grace, and hence only in the mode of worship, prayer, and adoration, in which we respond humbly and obediently to his divine initiative in making himself known to us personally and savingly through his Word as our Creator, Lord and Savior.

It is a form of the same scientific method that was held by Christians in the Early Church to apply to the understanding and interpretation of the Holy Scriptures which call for a deep seated change of mind, appropriate to the reality and nature of God's *Word* as it is mediated to us in and through the Scriptures. That is to say, the Holy Scriptures were to be interpreted objectively in accordance with the nature of the divine Realities and Activities to which they direct us. In them God has adapted his self-revelation to human language in such a way, that human statements in the Scriptures direct us beyond themselves to God, so that in seeking to understand and interpret the Scriptures as given us by God, the divine reality they mediate, the very Word of God himself, is not to be subordinated to the human word, but the human word to the divine reality to which they refer. Scientific method requires us, therefore, to give careful attention both to the human character of the Scriptures and to the transcendent Nature of God, but in so doing to take the Reality of God's self-revelation to us in the Scriptures so seriously that we look through the human word to the divine Reality of God's self-revealing Word mediated to us in and through the Scriptures. It was much the same relation that Christians found to obtain between the activity of natural scientists and the realities they seek to understand: when the scientist inquires into the nature of the contingent world, he does that not by looking at God but by looking away from him at the world, but when the theologian inquires into the nature of God, as he has revealed himself to us he does that not by looking at the nature of the world, which God created out of nothing, but by looking away from the world to its Creator. In both instances the scientist and the theologian seek to act strictly in accordance with the nature of the objective reality into which he inquires.

2) *Direct input.* Never in all the history of science has Christian theology had such a transforming impact on science as through *John Philoponos* of Alexandria in the sixth century. His was a biblical and Christocentric theology in which he developed the Christian conception of the creation of the universe out of nothing and sought to give an adequate account of its contingent rational order. Of particular importance for him was the Biblical teaching about the incarnation of the Creator Word of God in Jesus Christ, the Light of the world through whom all things were made, and of the intrinsic relation between the divine Word and the divine Light. Working with a distinction between uncreated Light and created light, he put forward a *theory of light* and a *theory of impetus*, which together overthrew the static inertial notions of Aristotelian science, and produced a dynamic understanding not only of sciences such as optics, physics, and meteorology, but of the unitary universe of heaven and earth. In the course of this transformation of classical science he advanced *relational conceptions of time and space*, defining them in terms of the dynamic of what he called "light force". This called for a new holistic way of thinking of real intelligible relations with which traditional Aristotelian and Euclidean logic, concerned with static patterns and relations, could not cope, which came under severe attack particularly from Aristotelian philosophers and scientists like Simplicius known in the Medieval world as "The Commentator". However, the overthrow of a static for a dynamic theory of light, and the transformation of physics it involved, was an astonishing anticipation of the role of light put forward by Clerk Maxwell and Einstein more than a thousand years later.

It should be added that in accordance with Philoponos' conception of the contingent nature of the universe and its rational order, as also in accordance with his doctrine of the creation of the world out of nothing freely through the Word of God incarnate in Jesus Christ, Philoponos would have nothing to with any attempt to argue logically from the nature of the world to the existence of God, for that would have meant that God is necessarily related to the world, and that would imply that the world was not freely created by him out of nothing, while nevertheless endowed with a form of rational order utterly distinct from God but dependent on him. While science transformed under the impact of Christian theology, points properly away from itself to God, that is because of the Christian theological input into understanding of its contingent nature.

The work of John Philoponos represents an outstanding instance of the direct cognitive *input of Christian beliefs* in the development of natural science. Of signal importance in it was the relation between the uncreated Light and Word of God, and created "light" and creaturely "word". This relation between light and word involved an *informational input* into scientific theory beyond what could be extracted by way of reflection upon the activity of the physical light in the cosmos by itself. Physical light was, and had to be, understood not merely through its empirical behavior, but through the bearing upon it of information which shaped its theoretical content. Expressed otherwise, it was through a "meta-relation" of light to "word", and above all to the Word of God, that it came to be understood and deployed by Philoponos in his transformation of science. It was thus through the cognitive content of his faith that Philoponos actually developed his epoch-making light theory and impetus theory. This raises for us the importance of what we call "information theory", and the need to take into account some sort of transcendent order, or "meta-plan", in developing scientific theory especially at boundaries between being and non-being. That is, of course, particularly clear today in respect of the human genome which is laden with more information than would fill a vast encyclopedia, and which by its astonishing complex nature could not have arisen in some sort of accidental or self-organisational way.

John Philoponos' development of dynamic science led to a significant *feed-back* into Christian theology, not in content but by way of developing its dynamic character in accordance with the redemptive activity of the incarnate Word of God. This had already been taking place, particularly through the thought of the great theologians, Athanasius and Cyril of Alexandria. Now, however, the interrelation between this theology and science, which had given rise to dynamic science, rebounded upon Philoponos' theology in respect of his scientific method and technical terms, giving them a more dynamic form. The crunch came when basic theological terms were given a *dynamic* slant in accordance with the dynamic nature of the realities to which they referred. That meant that they could not be interpreted in their classical literary sense, that is, as read in accordance with the meanings they had in classical Greek literature, and as read particularly through the twin spectacles of Plato and Aristotle. Thus crucial terms and expressions referring to the nature and oneness of the incarnate Son of God came under severe attack from the Byzantine Establishment. For example, when Philoponos cited Cyril's expression, "the one incarnate nature of the Word of God", and interpreted it holistically in accordance with his one dynamic reality and not analytically, he was accused of being a monophysite heretic - that is, one who denies that Christ was both divine and human - was anathematized, and his writings were banned, with the result that science, and the cognitive relation of theology to science, not least the cognitive input of theology in science, were obstructed until modern times. The rejection of Philoponos had the disastrous effect of allowing Aristotelian science, with its radical dualist outlook, and its inertial concept of God as the Unmoved Mover, and its logico-analytical modes of thought in theology and science, to overrun Western culture and to give rise to the dualist and deterministic conception of the world that stems from Galileo and Newton.

3) *Regulative impact.* In modern times there arose a new Philoponos, *James Clerk Maxwell*, a devout Christian believer, whose light theory and impetus theory together also gave rise to a *dynamical* way of scientific thinking, which

broke free from the kind of mechanistic science based on Newton's *Principia Mathematica*, and opened up the way with his dynamic field theory of light for the transformation of science through relativity and quantum theory. The decisive change came with the publication of Clerk Maxwell's epoch-making book, *A Dynamical Theory of the Electromagnetic Field*, 1864, which according to Einstein brought about the greatest change in the axiomatic basis of physics and correspondingly in our conception of reality. This was followed by Clerk Maxwell's two-volume work *A Treatise on Electricity and Magnetism* in 1873, which must be reckoned with Newton's *Principia Mathematica* as one of the two great works on which modern science rests.

Clerk Maxwell did not intrude theological ideas specifically or directly into his scientific theories, but the Christian faith deeply entrenched in his being exercised a *regulative role* in the choice and formation of his leading scientific concepts. Thus the cast of his mind, shaped through an intuitive apprehension of the relation of God to his creation, provided him with what he called "a fiducial point or standard of reference" for discriminating scientific judgments. It directed him to real ends external to himself, and to the kind of real objectivity he needed for critical scientific activity, not least in grasping and bringing to appropriate expression the intelligible relations inherent in nature. This called for a *holistic* rather than an analytic and abstractive way of thinking, in which he could let real dynamic relations have their full value, without being mauled by abstract Aristotelian logic which applies only to flat space and not, as Einstein showed, to space-time. Hence Clerk Maxwell inverted the current mathematical and scientific way of beginning with analytical particulars and building up the whole by synthesis, but made primary a mathematico-conceptual mode of interpreting dynamic realities and real ontological relations without distorting them. At the same time his Christian faith provided Clerk Maxwell with certain "analogical truths", root ideas, and fundamental conceptions, for which natural science could not account but which guided him in the scientific task of wedding thought with reality and developing appropriate ideas. He spoke of these as "modes of thought" and "physical truths" matched to the unveiling of processes inherent in nature, which called for a corresponding mode of "physical reasoning" and a "new mathesis in mathematics" particularly concerned with ontological relations of space and time relations.

Clerk Maxwell became convinced that "in a scientific point of view the *relation* is the most important think to know". The kind of relations he wanted to express and develop were not of a putative kind but real relations of an ontological kind inhering in reality, for the inter-relations of things are ontologically constitutive of what they really are. The relations between things, even of persons, belong to what they are. That was a conviction deeply rooted in Scottish theology and metaphysics which Clerk Maxwell was to call to his aid when again and again he failed to offer a satisfactory explanation of the behavior of the moving lines of force in the electromagnetic field in terms of Newtonian physics and mechanics. Thus when he developed an explanation of the behavior of electro-magnetic particles, in particular of the way in which light particles, relate ontologically and dynamically with one another moving at the speed of light, he came up with the concept of the *continuous dynamic field*, which had the effect of transforming the laws of classical Newtonian mechanics, and opening the way toward a new understanding of physical reality in terms of relativity and quantum theory. This was a revolutionary counterpart to the transformation of Aristotelian science by John Philoponos in the sixth century through the combination of light theory and impetus theory. It was not that Clerk Maxwell imported theological conceptions as such into his science, but rather that the pressure of his Christian understanding of God and his creation of the world led him to put forward new ideas and ways of thinking that transformed the basic structure of natural science, and were congenial to the Christian understanding of the universe of space and time. In other words, it was his basic Christian beliefs that prompted his new scientific thinking and exercised a *regulative* role in the choice and formation of his leading scientific concepts.

What, then, about the relation of *light* to *word*, created light to the uncreated Light and Word of God, the transcendent Source of all contingent order in the universe? It is to Clerk Maxwell that we owe the discovery that light has mathematical properties. Everything we know in the universe, macrocosmically or microcosmically, we learn from light signals, but their mathematical patterns have to be deciphered and coordinated with word in the formation of scientific theory and the development of knowledge. That is to say, as Philoponos taught, *information* is needed in understanding the of light and its divinely given dynamic role in the universe. Created light by its very nature, points away to the uncreated Light and Word of God, the ultimate ground of all rational order and the transcendent source of the information needed in the development of science. Philoponos and Clerk Maxwell together thus point us in seeking understanding of the universe toward some **meta-source** of knowledge or *meta-order* to guide our research and develop appropriate scientific theory. It is, I believe, along these lines that we may profitably think out for our generation the cognitive bearing of Christian belief upon the advance of scientific knowledge of the universe that God has made and within which his Word became incarnate in space and time. It is as we do that we will be able to develop adequately something like "the Theology of Sciences".

Made in the USA
San Bernardino, CA
03 August 2017